THE BEST WOMEN'S
STAGE MONOLOGUES 2018

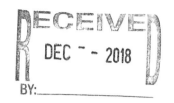

D0757455

THE BEST WOMEN'S STAGE MONOLOGUES 2018

Edited and with a Foreword

by Lawrence Harbison

SMITH AND KRAUS PUBLISHERS

A Smith and Kraus Book
177 Lyme Road, Hanover, NH 03755
editorial 603.643.6431 To Order 1.877.668.8680
www.smithandkraus.com

Manufactured in the United States of America

ISBN: 9781575259253

Library of Congress Control Number: 2329-2709

Typesetting and layout by Elizabeth E. Monteleone

Cover by Olivia Monteleone

For information about custom editions, special sales,
education and corporate purchases,
please contact Smith and Kraus at editor@smithandkraus.com or
603.643.6431.

ACKNOWLEDGEMENTS

Thanks to the following press agents for allowing me to see productions they represented during the 2017-2018 theatre season: Molly Barnett, Mike Borkowski, Scott Braun, Shane Brown, Philip Carruba, Melissa Cohen, Alexandra Cutler, Tom D'Ambrosio, Daniel Demello, Michelle Farabaugh, Glenna Freedman, David Gersten, David Gibbs, Whitney Gore, Karen Greco, Jackie Green, Kelly Guiod, Dale Heller, Richard Hillman, Ailsa Hoke, Judy Jacksina, Jessica Johnson, Michael Jorgenson, Alana Karpoff, Amy Kass, Amanda Kaus, Bridget Klapinski, Scott Klein, Richard Kornberg, Ron Lasko, Kevin McAnarney, Aaron Meier, Miguel Mendiola, Logan Metzler, Shayne Miller, Chelsea Nachman, Brett Charles, Emily Owens, Leslie Papa, Joe Perrotta, Matt Polk, Imani Punch, Jim Randolph, Philip Rinaldi, Lily Robinson, Katie Rosin, Matt Ross, Sam Rudy, Susan Schulman, Sarah Sgro, Paul Siebold, Rachael Singer, Jonathan Slaff, Don Summa, Don Summa, Joe Trentacosta, Wayne Wolfe, Samantha Wolfin, Molly Wyatt, John Wyczniewski, Billy Zavelson and Blake Zidell; and to the following literary agents who granted me rights to include their clients' work in this anthology: Beth Blickers, Jonathan Mills, Amy Wagner, Rachel Viola, Mark Orsini, Seth Glewen, Max Grossman, Amy Mellman, Di Glazer, Olivier Sultan, Rachel Taylor, Mark Subias, Antje Oegel, Susan Gurman, Leah Hamos and Ally Shuster.

Thanks, too, to Amy Marsh of Samuel French, Inc., Peter Hagan of Dramatists Play Service and Christopher Gould of Broadway Play Publishing for sending me plays to read.

And, thanks most of all to the playwrights who sent me their plays.

TABLE OF CONTENTS

FOREWORD

Here you will find a rich and varied selection of monologues for women from plays most of which were produced and/or published in the 2017-2018 theatrical season. Many are for younger performers (teens through 30s) but there are also some excellent pieces for older women as well. Some are comic (laughs), some are dramatic (generally, no laughs). Some are rather short, some are rather long. All represent the best in contemporary playwriting.

Several of the monologues are by playwrights whose work may be familiar to you, such as Don Nigro, Rinne Groff, Wendy MacLeod, John Cariani, Aaron Posner, Sarah Ruhl, Dominique Morisseau and Beau Willimon; others are by exciting up-and-comers such as Jacqueline Goldfinger, Deborah Zoe Laufer, C.S. Hanson, Tanya Saracho, Merridith Allen, Paola Lázaro, Susan Eve Haar, Susan Soon Hi Stanton and Chelsea Marcantel.

Many of the plays from which these monologues have been culled have been published and, hence, are readily available either from the publisher/licensor or from a theatrical book store such as the Drama Book Shop in New York. A few plays may not be published for a while, in which case contact the author or his agent to request a copy of the entire text of the play which contains the monologue which suits your fancy. Information on publishers/rights holders may be found in the Rights & Permissions section in the back of this anthology.

Break a leg in that audition! Knock 'em dead in class!

Lawrence Harbison

THE MONOLOGUES

ACTUALLY
Anna Ziegler

Dramatic
Amber Cohen, late teens - early twenties

Amber is addressing the audience, describing her first sexual experience, which, with or without her knowing, contributed to shaping her attitude and expectations around sex for years to come.

AMBER

Rachel had fallen asleep on the couch, and Zach was just like "Amber" and I was like "yeah?" and he asked if I wanted to see this app on his phone that's like an updated version of Angry Birds Star Wars and I said sure, but really he just wanted me to come sit next to him because once I was there he kind of touched my wrist and I froze and of course he knew. I mean, really he'd probably known for years. And he stands and kind of pulls me up with him, and we go to his room and he's kinda stumbly drunk and I am completely sober and we fall onto the bed and he is not exactly gentle with me but I don't really mind; the next day I get a UTI and it hurts so bad, but I don't know that right now and eventually he takes his fingers out of me and squeezes one of my boobs really hard, and I moan a little because I think that's what people do but he puts his finger to his mouth like I've made this faux pas by making a sound, a gesture I remember at least subconsciously because now I am always silent during sex, always always, like you practically don't know I'm there, and then he climbs on top of me and sticks it in. And the whole time, which isn't a long time, I keep thinking "I got into college today" which, in conjunction with what's happening right now, makes me feel like a…yeah, like a different person, I guess. And when he's done he grunts a little, like this sound is just getting pushed out of him and it's not exactly a happy sound, but still I feel weirdly privileged—and in all honesty, grown up—to know what Zach Lieberman sounds like when he comes.

For information on this author,
click on the WRITERS tab at www.smithandkraus.com.

ACTUALLY
Anna Ziegler

Dramatic
Amber Cohen, late teens - early twenties

In this direct address to the audience, Amber is describing her first date with Tom, the guy on whom she has a big crush in the first weeks of college. Before the date, Amber revealed to Tom that she sees him everywhere—at the gym, in class, on the quad, and even in the ice cream parlor on campus.

AMBER

The funny thing, or maybe it was just weird, was that I'd never actually seen him at the ice cream place. As soon as I said it I knew it was wrong; I was just running at the mouth the way I do sometimes, and sometimes as a result not everything I say is one hundred percent wholly and completely true. I mean, maybe it's just that ice cream is never far from my mind. Or maybe I just wanted it to be true but either way we do end up getting ice cream the next day and he offers to buy mine, which even though I demur because I'm the product of feminists who worked really hard to have the right to buy their own ice cream, the offer means we're on a real date, right? Me and 'Thomas Anthony,' who, I mean, even his name is hot, and who knows, maybe he's gonna be my first real boyfriend, not counting my camp boyfriend, which in all honesty was a relationship based almost entirely on correspondence. Anyway I can't really believe it, and I'm trying not to think about all the other things I should be doing, like seriously the call of those books stacked on my desk is deafening, and also I didn't work out as hard as I usually do this afternoon, I don't know why, and now this ice cream that I can't help but eat all of is gonna make me fat, I can feel myself getting fatter as I eat it, not that I have eating issues, I mean, I don't, aside from the way all girls have eating issues, which is that we think about what we eat 100% of the time and always wanna kill ourselves.

For information on this author,
click on the WRITERS tab at www.smithandkraus.com.

AIRNESS
Chelsea Marcantel

Dramatic
Nina, twenty-thirty

Nina, new to the world of competitive air guitar, is confronted by her ex-boyfriend — National Champion D Vicious. In a burst of anger, Nina fills Vicious in on the real reason she has begun to research, compete, and strive for air guitar greatness.

NINA

I loved you! I loved our band and our apartment and our life. I loved you. But when you started to get really good at air guitar, you checked out of our relationship. You bailed out of nowhere.

(frustrated with herself)

Oooh, this is your *favorite*! This moment when I feel stupid and say idiotic things and you have all the power. You *love* this. You broke up our REAL band, you broke up our REAL relationship, for what? To fuck somebody else's wife and spend every night in shitty bars with people who think you're cool because you're the best at IMAGINARY GUITAR? To play PRETEND with a gaggle of second-rate UNFUCKABLE LOSERS who couldn't be contributing members of society if they tried? THIS is your kingdom? THIS is where you're god? You ruined my REAL LIFE, and you get to be happy in PRETEND LAND? FUCK THAT, and FUCK YOU.

(she takes a breath, is calmer)

I'm not doing this to get you back. When someone breaks your heart, you find out what they love most in the whole world. Then you take it from them.

For information on this author,
click on the WRITERS tab at www.smithandkraus.com.

ALL THE RAGE
Joshua James

Seriocomic
Lisa, 30s

After a nice handsome man buys Lisa a drink, she shares how she really feels.

LISA

Okay. *(Very brief pause.)* Have you ever felt like killing somebody, I mean REALLY felt like actually killing somebody? It doesn't have to be anyone you know, it could be just Joe-Schmoe on the street, you know? You ever just see somebody and get the urge to hit them, you know, over the head with something hard and heavy? Or have you ever been standing in line behind somebody at the grocery store, stuck behind a very loud person with nowhere to run and she's complaining to the check-out person and she's usually complaining about something completely beyond the power of the clerk to do anything about, say she's mad because macaroni's not on sale this week, it was on sale last week why can't it be on sale this week too and you look at this person standing in line bitching about NOTHING and you just want to rip her arm off and beat her to death with it. Just hammer her over her head with her own arm, screaming over and over "SHUT UP SHUT UP SHUT UP! IT'S JUST A COUPON SO SHUT UP!" That ever happen to you? And the way some people get off the bus or train, run into you and not have the common fucking decency to say "excuse me," and sometimes they won't even look at you, like they couldn't be bothered, and it makes you just want to take out your apartment keys, go up to them and stab them right in the eyes! And especially people with cell phones, I am to the point now where anytime I see someone with a cell phone I want to take it away from them and make them EAT IT whole, it's like you can't go anywhere without having someone else's boring fucking private conversation forced down your throat! I was standing in line at the movie theater and I was forced to listen to some asshole discuss the results of his proctology exam with his doctor! I wanted to take the phone away from him and shove it straight up his ass! I was even on a date last week, we were out at dinner and he took a call right in the middle of the appetizer that lasted halfway through our main course! And it wasn't even anything important, he was setting up a squash match with one of his buddies! And I had to sit there and listen to him josh around with his pal, like I had nothing better to do! You know what I did, you wanna know what I did? I I waited until we were finished eating, because it was a wonderful filet mignon and I didn't want to waste it, excused myself, went to the ladies room, called him from there on his cell phone and screamed "HEY ASSHOLE! DON'T EVER CALL ME AGAIN YOU SELF-IMPORTANT CONDESCENDING PRICK WITH TOO MUCH MONEY AND NOT ENOUGH HAIR! ASSHOLE ASSHOLE ASSHOLE! And then I left. I wanted to do more, I did, I wanted to really hurt him. But I had to settle for just screaming at him. People, people just drive me crazy sometimes, sometimes I want to crush them all, they're so stupid. I think I'm kind of angry. Do you think I'm kind of angry?

For information on this author,
click on the WRITERS tab at www.smithandkraus.com.

AMY AND THE ORPHANS
Lindsey Ferrentino

Comic
Kathy, 20s-early 40s

Kathy is a loud-mouthed, fun-loving, over-sharing caretaker at a group home for adults with down syndrome. She is eight months pregnant, but still makes sure to take her smoke breaks (even though she doesn't smoke). She is the walking embodiment of Long Island, New York. The audience shouldn't know to whom she is speaking for most of the monologue, until it is revealed that she is sharing all of this with a convenience store worker at a rest stop.

KATHY

My dumbass boyfriend— he wants to host a big-ass baptism, we're not even married, but God forbid we miss *this* fuckin' sacrament! So now we're pickin' God parents which is the sickest shit, you know, it's like *WHO outta you people will care for my baby if I can't.* I'm like, "My best friend *obviously.*" He's like "Your best friend's a pot head." I'm like— "- well, point taken." My dumb-ass boyfriend's got two sisters. One's happily married, big house, I'm like let's pick her, she cooks a good ziti and buys me gifts, but problem is— she already got kids of her own. Lemme tell ya, two kids, close in age, you got your hands full. Then he's got this LOSER sister who nobody picks. Nobody picks her for anything. The good sister didn't pick her for either of her two kids, but my dumb-ass boyfriends like *"we gotta pick her, nobody picks her!"* I'm like, "there's a FUCKIN' reason *why*!" She lives with your fuckin' father and take how she treats those dogs. Their dad watches dogs, ya know, for extra money. I dunno, he loves dogs. He's like— gay for dogs. Well this asshole dog comes in the house, shits on the dad's sofa when the dad's not home. My dumb-ass boyfriend wants to hose it off, but the loser sister says we should leave the shit to teach their father a lesson. Lemme tell you this. It's HIS house. She don't pay rent. He takes in extra dogs to support his loser daughter and she's gonna let the dog shit ferment? Uh-uh. My dumb-ass boyfriends draggin' the whole couch outside, gettin' the hose, she's screaming in the drive way, *"LEAVE THE SHIT ON THE CUSHION TO TEACH DAD TO RESPECT HIMSELF!"* I'm all *yeah,* Rosario, if you think that's who I want to care for my baby, you're outta your goddamn mind. —What're these, beef jerkys on sale? I'll take four. And fill her up on pump thirteen. *Oh God, what to do...* Look. I'm not sayin' there are only bad people in the world. 'Cause there are a lotta good ones too. And most of us in between. But as my dumb ass boyfriend always says: Beggars cannot be choosers. If it ain't YOU raisin' that baby... who knows *what* you're gonna get.

For information on this author,
click on the WRITERS tab at www.smithandkraus.com.

AND THEN THEY FELL
Tira Palmquist

Dramatic
Cal, 17, transgender

Phoenix. Downtown. The streets are quiet, almost deserted – and it has begun to rain. Cal, angry, finally makes it clear to his new friend Jordan why he knows exactly how hard it is to be a teenager on the streets, and how hard it is to go home.

CAL

Three months ago, I came home to find all my stuff on the front porch. No warning, no explanation — just a pile of my clothes, my stuff for school. The day before, I'd asked my Dad to call me Cal. I told him I'd never felt like a girl, that I couldn't be his little girl, not any more. I remember when I told him he was looking out the front window like he was watching the neighbors doing something shifty. You know, this frown, his mouth all pursed up and tense. He said, "Well, what's that mean? You gay?" "No, I'm not gay," I said. "I'm just not Callista. I never have been." I told him I'd done research, and that I'd talked to a counselor at school, and that I wanted to think about transitioning, to start testosterone therapy. He just — walked out of the room. He left the house without saying a word. I thought, well, he'll get over it. He'll be OK. But... The next day, after school, there it was. My life. On the porch. And the door was locked. I knocked. I yelled. I rang the doorbell. Finally, he opened the door, with this look on his face — a look I'd never seen. He was a different fucking person. "Dad," I said. "What the hell are you doing?" He said, "I don't know who you are, but you're not my child." *(Pause)* I tried to take my stuff inside, and he beat the crap out of me. He said, "I'd rather see you dead than have you set one foot inside my house again."

For information on this author,
click on the WRITERS tab at www.smithandkraus.com.

ANIMAL
Clare Lizzimore

Seriocomic
Rachel, 30s

Rachel is in a session with her therapist, Stephen. She is there because her husband has become concerned about her depression. Stephen has suggested that she "do something nice for yourself." Maybe give herself a face masque.

RACHEL

Oh so you mean, put some bubbles in the bath? Dress in a white robe, little white peep toe slippers, and a face masque, and think of smiley things? You want to know something they didn't teach you at school? They didn't teach you that it's women in the movies that do that, and that real women step in shit on way home, and spend the journey doing scrape-y sideways walking to try and ditch the stench. But. Inevitably. It gets stuck in the grooves and you're actually, with all that shuffling, you're grinding it into the soles. And then, you know what happens then? Your bags split as you're crossing the threshold, so your shopping's all rolling about in the dirt as your kicking it in the house, with those shoes, the ones with the shit. And then you get in *(Beat)* and there's a power cut. So you eat your dinner in the dark, after cleaning your shoes in the sink, and they're there on the counter sodden and fucked up with the memory of shit and you think, at least the shoe has its double. *(Beat)* So now they're sat there, stinking, but smug, smug cause there's two. And you're just one. Until your husband comes home. And even then, laying there in the dark, the shoes have it better. 'Cause at least they're a match.

For information on this author,
click on the WRITERS tab at www.smithandkraus.com.

ANIMAL
Clare Lizzimore

Dramatic
Rachel, 30s

Rachel, a very unhappy woman, is speaking to her husband, Tom.

RACHEL

Did you always know you'd marry me? At school? I knew I'd marry you. For better or worse. I said to you 'I love your eyes.' You said 'I love your wrists.' 'Wrists.' I said. 'That's a funny thing to love.' You said 'well loves a funny thing.' You started a list of loveable things. 'The indent under your nose, what's it called?' you said. 'Philtrum' I said. 'Philtrum. Yes. Philtrum', 'It's not symmetrical, you know that don't you?' I said, 'I was wondering if you knew that?' It was the first thing I noticed about you, when you arrived, everyone else thought you were like this God, like this mysterious God, and they flocked to you like chickens to corn. But when I saw you. I just thought his face is wonky. *(Tiny beat)* and that's what made you like me, isn't it? I was the fox, in a pen of silly little chickens, I was dangerous cause I saw you for your flaws. Nowhere to hide. The ugly truth. I looked it up. Philtrum. It has no function. In the womb, in utero, the two sides of your face develop independently of one another and then at some point, before birth, they join in the middle. *(Beat)* Your face didn't fuse properly. Have you ever thought about that? The ugly truth. What's my ugly truth Tom? Do you know? Do you? My brain. Why's that never on the list?

For information on this author,
click on the WRITERS tab at www.smithandkraus.com.

ANIMAL
Clare Lizzimore

Dramatic
Rachel, 37

Rachel's therapist, Stephen, believes she is suffering from post-partum psychosis. They are talking about a disturbing dream she has had.

RACHEL

I think my scarecrow man had a scarecrow wife. And I think they had a baby, who was made of the best and softest straw. And the scarecrow wife said, I don't know how to love this baby, fragile made of sticks. So she bought it a rose. But the scarecrow man said, what do you think that is? And she said. Love. But he said. That's not love, scarecrow wife. Can't you think of anything better? *(Beat)* So she thought. Yes. Of course I can. So off she went, slowly making her way down the stairs, out the house, and down the garden. But I don't think she's ever coming home. Cause she's still looking for the thing. The thing that she can bring back and say there. *(Beat)* There. That's love. Right there. That's safety. That's kindness. That's protection. That's a promise. That we don't have to live in shit, that the rich don't just get richer, that the bullies don't win. That you can be exactly what you want to be. Promise. I brought you into a world that's fair, and just, and equal. (Beat) and she's wracking her brains out there. And all the while the baby made of sticks and straw, she's growing, she's tall; she's a beautiful straw girl. And she's clever. She passed all her exams at scarecrow school. And you know, she's the most beautiful, beautiful, pianist. And sometimes when the scarecrow wife is crawling like an animal, in the dirt, looking for the meaning of it all. *(Beat)* She thinks she can hear this sound, and it's so beautiful that it makes her cry. And then it hits her, hard, in the chest. The simple truth. The very thing she was looking for. And then she laughs in anger. And rage. And spite. But she's lost in the woods so no one ever sees her. And her husband – he's looking in all the wrong places. In the light. In the fields. In the sun.

For information on this author,
click on the WRITERS tab at www.smithandkraus.com.

Lawrence Harbison

APROPOS OF NOTHING
Greg Kalleres

Comic
Lily, 30s-40s

Martin & Lily have always been considered the gold standard of marriage among their friends. But, lately, Lily has secretly begun to wonder if they're lives have become too "cliché." In this scene, Lily is shocked when her close friend, Rebecca, casually reveals that she's never liked Martin — and it touches a nerve.

LILY

I will remind you that you are talking about my *husband.* And one of the reasons I married him was so I wouldn't have to ask myself anything anymore. See, I never have to wonder if the person I'm with is interesting enough or smart enough or makes me happy enough! I don't have question myself about his taste in shoes or why he talks to himself in the bathroom, or why only has seven songs on his iPod shuffle! Two of which are the same Hooty and the Blowfish song! And I don't have to drive myself crazy wondering if it's odd that he smells his hands before he eats or that he keeps his underwear around one ankle during sex so he always knows where it is. Or if this is the man I should have children with! And if they too will have sex with their underwear around one ankle! And best of all, I don't have to stay up nights asking myself if there is someone else out there who would make me happier or inspire me more! Someone who could make me laugh and care and want in a way I never have! You have any idea what it's like not to have to ask those horrible questions!? It's amazing! It's the reason I am blissfully happy you are miserable! BECAUSE WE ARE MARTIN & FUCKING LILY!

For information on this author,
click on the WRITERS tab at www.smithandkraus.com.

THE ARSONISTS
Jacqueline Goldfinger

Dramatic
M, 20s

A daughter finally reveals the truth about her mother's death to her father.

M

The night before her funeral. You ripping out yourself in the woods. I sneaked over to the funeral home. Crawled into the coffin. I crawled in, all eight years squished between the smooth velvet and her cold arm. And I reached up to hold her face. to give her a kiss and say I love you and I'm sorry and if I did this, if I did, if this was my fault, I'm sorry, it was probably my fault. It was probably my, because I was a ... let's be truth now I was a pain in the ass. And I's so sorry. And to come on back home. I'll be good. But when I reached up to hold, to kiss, I couldn't get to her face. I couldn't because there wasn't no face there.

(Moves to stroke mother's face but can't.)

There wasn't, There was a chin, And a mouth, And a nose, And bandages. And I couldn't reach, or untie or unfold, or fold with or to or between us, I couldn't, I tried. I did. I'm sorry, Momma, I'm trying but I can't reach you. And so I gave her a kiss on the cheek and snuggled down underneath her arm. And the next morning the burial man find me and he says, "You can't be here young lady. You a bad young lady. Bad girl. Bad." And he shoved me off. But in that long last night, I held her. I held her and I knew it was just gonna be me and you, Daddy. Me and you, forever. No one else. No one else to cry or scream or ... Any of it. Just us. And now there are pieces missing from both of you. And I don't want to find 'em. Because it only means you'll go away.

THE ART OF THE FUGUE
Don Nigro

Seriocomic
Felicia, 18

Felicia is a gifted and beautiful pianist who is spending the summer with her friend Jane at Jane's family home in a small town in east Ohio while the two prepare for their upcoming performing tour in Europe. Jane's brothers Jamie and Andrew are home from World War I, two troubled young men. Andrew keeps trying to sleep with her, but Jamie, the kinder of the brothers, is deeply love with her. Here Felicia, who is usually more guarded, opens up to Jamie one night about her background. There is a part of her that has always craved the quiet, easy going small town family atmosphere that she's immersed in this summer, and she is attracted to Jamie and the stable life he could give her. But she is also ambitious, emotionally troubled, and drawn towards the sort of self-destructive behavior that will eventually lead her fall into a much darker relationship with Andrew. This is as close as she will let herself get to Jamie before pulling away.

FELICIA

My father was a big man in the stockyards. He got rich taking cattle to the slaughterhouse. Mother was artistic. She loved music and literature and wanted to shelter me from father's vulgarity. She hated the blood under his fingernails. She lived mostly on apples. He would drink and scream at her that it was his god damned vulgarity that paid for the god damned piano lessons and the god damned piano and the clothes on my god damned back. But most of the time he didn't shout. He made ironic comments, like cutting off little pieces of her flesh. I can't imagine them ever having made love. He courted her, she said, with great tenderness and persistence, as if she were the Holy Grail. She was excited by his strength and practical capabilities. He was good at making things, selling things, repairing things, killing things. He referred to music as 'that god damned noise.' Sometimes he'd come home drunk late at night and bring me balloons. I hate balloons. My childhood was ecstatic. I played Bach every day. Nothing else really mattered. Although after my father choked to death on roast beef—the revenge of the cows, mother said—I did go a little wild. He dropped dead at the dinner table, and the cuckoo came out of the clock thirteen times. He'd just fixed it the day before, and he was so proud of himself, he had to talk about it while he was eating. Mother was greatly relieved, I think. And even though money was scarce after the roast beef killed Papa, she insisted I keep up with my piano lessons, even during her last illness. I got into the Conservatory just before she died. Boarded with deeply stupid relations in Cleveland. Uncle Bud was always trying to show me his penis, until one day, I slammed the lid of the piano on it. That discouraged him a bit. They threw me out, so I lied about my age and moved into a girls' boarding house. Jane was my only friend there. Being here is heaven. This porch. This wonderful old rackety house. All these brothers and sisters and all your cousins across the street. I don't know how you can all possibly keep track of each other. It's paradise, really. I wish I could stay here forever.

THE ART OF THE FUGUE
Don Nigro

Dramatic
Felicia, 18

Felicia is a beautiful and brilliantly talented pianist who is spending the summer with her friend Jane at the small town Ohio home of Jane's family, preparing for their first concert tour of Europe in the fall. She is a troubled girl, orphaned and abused, who has been pleasantly surprised by how much she likes the quiet Ohio summer with a big family of brothers and sisters and cousins in a small town. Jane's brother Jamie has fallen hopelessly in love with Felicia, but Felicia has chosen to let another brother, Andrew, seduce her. Here she is trying, in her own way, to gently explain to Jamie that she is not interested in a serious relationship with anybody, and prefers casual sex with Andrew, who is mostly interested in her because he hates Jamie. Felicia is trying to be kind to Jamie, and is actually probably a good deal more attracted to him than she wants to admit to herself, but all through this speech she is aware that she is ripping out Jamie's heart.

FELICIA

He is so angry at you. Not just once in a while, like normal brothers, if there is such a thing as normal brothers, but all the time. He feels like no matter what he does, he'll never measure up. He really does hate you very, very much. I think it's that capacity to hate so deeply that makes him so attractive. He's still carrying around every bit of that childhood anger. The war's just brought it closer to the surface. What do you think he's going to do to me? Because whatever it is, he's probably already done it. We've done pretty much everything you can do that's legal, and a couple of things that probably aren't, at least in this part of Ohio. What? Why are you looking at me like that? Are you shocked? Oh, poor boy. So in love with me. Don't be ashamed. It's perfectly understandable. But I'm not the answer. I'm just here to rehearse for my actual life, which is waiting for me out there in the autumn. Although I've got to confess, as much as I thought I'd be bored into absolute shrieking lunacy by now, trapped out here in the middle of east Ohio nowhere, the truth is, I feel more at home here than I ever felt anywhere. It's so nice. The children of two brothers, living across the street from one another all their lives in a pretty little small town in Ohio, all growing up together in one great wonderful herd. I've never had any real sense of family. There really is a part of me that doesn't want to leave. But that's ridiculous. We've got to be ready by autumn. Everything depends on it. And Bach is a harsh master. You can't just give him part of yourself. It's everything or nothing. I can't afford any distractions. Andrew is a release of tension. I hope you understand.

THE ART OF THE FUGUE
Don Nigro

Dramatic
Felicia, 21

Felicia is a brilliant and beautiful but troubled pianist who is touring Europe with her best friend Jane and Jane's two brothers, Jamie, who is in love with her, and Andrew, who she's been sleeping with. Here, it's four in the morning, and Jamie has heard her practicing the Bach fugues she plays in her concerts every night. She has become totally obsessed with these demanding and intricate pieces, and can't stop playing them, and Jamie is very concerned about her. There is abuse in her past, and she has chosen the brother who is increasingly cruel to her over the one who is good to her. Here she tries to explain to Jamie why she can't bring herself to love him. She is a tormented person and her life is spinning out of control.

FELICIA

Andrew I understand. Or, if I don't, it really doesn't matter. But people like you scare the hell out of me. And I've taught myself never to be afraid of anything. Except for balloons. When I was a little girl, there was this man who used to come around selling balloons. He looked like a goat. He even smelled like a goat. But I wasn't so much afraid of him as of the balloons. The texture of the balloons against your face. I used to have dreams that there were balloons clinging to my face and I couldn't get them off. They explode and the flesh ends up plastered on your face like the skin of a corpse. And when they're partially deflated, the way they feel against your neck. In my dream, the balloon man takes me into his caravan wagon. He has long, dirty fingernails and he touches my face.

It's still the only thing I'm really afraid of. Balloons, and you. I really should love you, shouldn't I? You're the only person I can talk to about things like that. You're very good to me. More than I deserve, usually. It's not that I take you for granted. It's just that you make me so nervous sometimes I think my head's going to explode. Sometimes I ask myself, do I not love you just because you love me? I don't know, and I don't want to know. The thing is, inside the music, everything is calm, well ordered. Even the passion is well ordered. Even when it's so complex and relentless you can't follow it. It's not that I know who I am when I'm inside the music. It's that I just disappear into the sound. Into the patterns. And it doesn't matter anymore. I disappear into the labyrinth of the patterns. That's what I want to do more than anything. Disappear. On a good night, I almost disappear completely. You really should get the hell away from me. Someday I'm going to get you killed.

THE ART OF THE FUGUE
Don Nigro

Dramatic
Felicia, 21

Felicia is a beautiful and brilliant pianist who's been touring Europe with great success playing "The Art of the Fugue" by J. S. Bach. But she is a very troubled young woman with abuse in her past, and she has been slowly coming apart mentally. Here she is speaking to her friend Jamie, who loves her, and who is trying to help her. He has just come upon his brother Andrew, who she's been sleeping with, physically abusing her, and has been trying to persuade her to get out of this increasingly abusive relationship before it's too late. But she can't seem to free herself, and retreats further into Bach's music, which has become for her a kind of living metaphor for her increasing despair and madness.

FELICIA

Do you know what I think about more and more now? I think of that summer evening on the porch with you. I was so cruel. And you told me I wasn't a terrible person. I think that's when I was certain I could never love you. I mean, how could anybody love a person that stupid? And yet I almost did love you, on a number of occasions. But then a voice in my head would remind me, no, mustn't do that. We must only love what kills us. That's the rule. That's the pattern. All fugues are a kind of loom that weaves patterns like a rug. Sometimes I imagine my life as a piece of music. It's a fugue which is also a room full of mirrors, like a funhouse. A fugue, mirrors, a labyrinth, sex: name four things you can get lost in. Music calls up demons. It's not an accident that genius, inspiration, is related to the daimon that whispered to Socrates and got him killed. There is resonance, and there is reflection, diminution, augmentation, and inversion—backwards and sideways, like a crab. If you seek, you will discover, but not what you were looking for. Seeking the answer to one question, you find the answer to another one, and it's probably something you very much didn't want to know. The fugues take you on a journey farther and farther away, filling you with a deeper and deeper longing for two contradictory things: both to find the solution to the problem, the center of the labyrinth, but also to find your way back home, to where you started. Recursion is nesting and variations on nesting, like Russian dolls. But what if you have no home? Maybe at the center of the labyrinth you'll find the garden that is home. Or maybe you'll find the monster that eats you. But whatever is at the center, or whether there is any center or not, once you're lost inside the fugue, there is no escape.

BABY SCREAMS MIRACLE
Clare Barron

Dramatic
Cynthia, 26

Cynthia has been estranged from her family for several years. But after a freak storm hits their small town in the Pacific Northwest, she travels back home to make amends. This monologue is a sort of ecstatic religious conversion that happens in the middle of the night. She speaks to her family, and also, to God.

CYNTHIA

I might be freaking out more than I should be. I just need God right now more than ever! I am going through some tough times. I am just so full of rage and sickness and despair about *everything everything*. I cry all the time. I cry every day. I just keep talking shit about people even though I want to stop talking shit about people. I tell myself I'm going to stop talking shit about people and then I just keep doing it. I keep talking shit. Please help me to stop. I'm just filled with rage. I don't know why. Like everyday everyday *ARRRRG* like I'm walking down the street and I just want to rip out people's assholes because of the way they walk, or how slow they walk, or because they keep commenting on everything, commenting on the sun and the weather and the flowers and the dresses in the window and I just want them to shut the fuck up because they're ruining it for me by talking about it. Because it's all ugly when they say it. And I know it's lame to feel that way but I can't help it because I'm full of rage. All the time. For as long as I can remember. I'm just full of rage. Because *everything everything* is lies and *everything everything* is exhausting and every tiny good thing you build for yourself takes so much work and so much sacrifice and nobody else even cares and the amount of sadness in the world and the amount of stupid stupid dumb dumb obligation and everything is lies but you don't realize it until you're a grown up and it's too late to change anything because the lies have grown into you and grown into your skin and you can't be separated from the lies like those people who have a metal stake in their brains and you can't take the metal stake out or they'll die so they just have to live with a metal stake in their brains for the rest of their life and everybody's walking around like that and you're just supposed to keep going and keep pretending And everyone thinks I'm a bitch but actually I'm just really easily intimidated and I don't know how to talk to people and I'm actually really shy and I don't hear things that well like actually I think I'm losing my hearing and so sometimes I don't hear the things that people say to me and so I just don't know how to respond so I just mouth words, I don't even say them I just mouth them, like "thank you" like on the street like some guy asks me what time it is and I just mouth the words "thank you" because I don't know what's going on and then he thinks I'm a bitch because I don't tell him the time but actually I'm just intimidated and feeling vulnerable and I feel vulnerable all the time. I cry all the time. And Arthur called me because he wanted to move the wedding to the summer and I thought he was maybe going to cancel it but actually he just wanted to do it in the summer and I got so scared that he was leaving me that I just started shitting in a plastic bag I couldn't even make it to the bathroom I just grabbed a plastic bag from off the floor and started shitting in it in my bedroom while he was on the phone and all he was saying was that we should get married in August and my body just started shitting because I was so scared that everything was ending and I would be all alone. I just need something to hold onto. I just need something to hold onto. Jesus Christ God please help me. Please just be with me.

BAD NEWS
Joshua James

Comic
Meryl, 20s

Meryl has just informed her buttoned down and very calm husband that she's had an affair. And not only that, there's more...

MERYL

Basically, I've had sex with nearly everyone you see while you're at work. And your brother. And also the boy that delivers the morning paper, he just turned fourteen. But before you lose complete control, there's more. I wrecked your car, your treasured Jaguar, I got high and totaled it last night. Actually, that's not true, although I was high, I wasn't driving. See, I had to let the paperboy drive, he's been dying to drive it and I promised him that once he got his learner's permit I would let him. I had to let him drive the car otherwise he was going to tell his mother that he and I were showering together every afternoon. So he was driving and while he was driving I was … servicing him, I guess you could say, servicing him orally, and he got so excited during said servicing that he ran right into the back of a school bus. That's why I didn't come home last night, I was in jail for molesting a minor. The kid's still in the hospital in critical condition. But there's more. I mortgaged the house and sold your motorcycle in order to make bail. I plan on skipping bail, so start looking for another place to live. Oh, that reminds me, you're flat broke. I emptied your savings accounts, cashed in all the CD's and T-bills and emptied your 401K. I did this last week, unfortunately, before I knew I was going to need bail money. I spent the money on Botox treatments for my thighs, they really needed the work, and all the rest on heroin, I've recently developed something of a habit, by the way you need to get an HIV test, I forgot to tell you. There's more. Your dog Skippy didn't run away, I had him put to sleep, I didn't like the way he was looking at me so I had him put him down. Actually, that's not true, I didn't have him put down, it costs a lot of money to put a dog to sleep, like about two hundred bucks, so instead I gave him to some farmer who killed him by hitting him over the head with a shovel. That way only costs five bucks. Oh, that reminds me, your mother didn't pass away peacefully in her sleep at the rest home. I smothered her with a pillow and then sold all of her vital organs on the black market. Also, I've been lying to you, my real name isn't Meryl, my real name is Mayreagon-noyustof and I'm here illegally from Lebanon.

For information on this author,
click on the WRITERS tab at www.smithandkraus.com.

BE HERE NOW
Deborah Zoe Laufer

Dramatic
Bari, 40s-50s

Bari's always been a bit of an angry, depressed misanthrope. And losing her job teaching nihilism in New York to work at the local fulfillment center in her rural hometown has sent her into despair. But lately her recurring headaches manifest bizarre, ecstatic, almost religious experiences, and they're changing her entire view of life. She's almost... happy! When she finds out they're also killing her, she must decide whether it's better to live a short, joyful life, or risk a lifetime of misery. And she must also ask herself... what's it all for anyway? In her new state, Bari has fallen in love with Mike, but is it real?

BARI

I want to feel this way. I love you. But is it really *me*? I don't know. Would I feel this way if there were no seizures? Probably not. And even if I did, would it just be because you're this brilliant artist? *Are* you this brilliant artist or do I just think you're a brilliant artist because of the seizures? Or, do I just think you're a brilliant artist because you're a MacArthur genius? Am I that shallow — I wouldn't be interested in you if you were just some guy making things out of garbage even though I see that they're remarkable? Maybe. Or, would I *just* be interested in you because you make these extraordinary things out of garbage, and I'm interpreting that as being *you*, when it's really just the thing you do. Like Wagner. You could be a Nazi, and I'm just blown away by your art, you know? I mean, I barely know you. As you said. And then, what if you were really really interested in *me*? Like, what if you told me *you* loved *me* last night? Would I still be interested in you? No, I'd be freaked out. But is it *just* your indifference that's appealing? No. No. Maybe I'm in love with you because the sex was so good and my brain is addled by oxytocin. And maybe the sex was so good because my brain is addled by the seizures. Before I had the seizures, I wouldn't have taken you home, and I wouldn't have had sex with you and I wouldn't have been flooded with neurochemicals and I wouldn't have seen your artwork, and I wouldn't have fallen in love with you. Am I in love with you? Yes. Am I me? I don't know. Am I actually the awful person I was before the seizures? Or is this who I really am, and the seizures have let me be the person I was meant to be? And if this is who I really am, who I was meant to be, will I still be this person if the seizures are taken away?

BLOOD AT THE ROOT
Dominique Morisseau

Dramatic
Toria, late teens, African-American

*Toria is a budding journalist, furious with the editor
of her high school newspaper because he won't print
an article she wrote because it's too controversial.*

TORIA

Justin, I'm tryin' to be a journalist. In real life. Do you get that? In real life! Not in some pretend lil' high school basement where the most interesting thang in print is whether or not we're having fake horsemeat on the lunch menu or who in God's name among the popular and stuck-up is gonna win Prom King and Queen. I am not interested in whether or not the auditorium gets a fresh coat of paint before December or whether or not the football team wins a single game this year. I am not interested in these pathetic little trifles that make up our sad existence as sheltered brats this side of the Mason Dixon line. I am interested in the true art of journalism. I want to tell the stories everybody else at this school and in this town is too pussy to cover. Like how many girls at this school have covered up their abortions because their parents are too primitive to allow a sex-ed course that isn't taught by 80-year-old Mrs. Wellsley who wouldn't know how to model puttin' on a condom if she had a 10-foot penis statue right in front of her. Or how about the number of boys on the football team who'd rather be dating each other than all the girls they swap semen with. But because we're so anti-homo they take it out on every chick at Cedar High and that's why the number of relationship violence is like sky high right now. Or like how about the fact that none of the black students on campus hardly ever hang out with any of the white students on campus or vice versa because we're

all a bunch of racist pricks. While every other delusional student at this school is networkin' on facebook or bloggin' about
what colleges they wanna go to, you're workin' on some new
colors to the layout. You're changin' the font from Times New
Roman to Comic Sans and that's really gonna make everybody
lose their shit and run to pick up a fuckin' paper! Just print
my fuckin' article. It's about protecting yourself and having a
healthy teen sex life. Did you even read it carefully? Or did you
get so excited at the word "birth control" that you skeeted on
yourself before you could finish? (Beat) It's our senior year. I
want to cover somethin' amazin'. Just once. Just to leave my
handprint here, y'know? You've got to understand what that
means. Aren't you sick of just bein' invisible at this place? I
don't want this year to be like every other one, y'know? Where
folks like us get lost forever into this abyss of nobodies because we're the only ones who know we're alive. Still waitin'
on this place to give back, y'know? These past three years I
ain't done nothin' but give and give to this hellhole, and it ain't
hardly reaped nothin'. But I decided this year I can finally find
a purpose for what I am at this school. I'm an investigator. And
I can't leave this year without fully definin' what I am. This is
the year I can etch myself into stone. Be a journalist. That's
what I want Justin. Don't you?

For information on this author,
click on the WRITERS tab at www.smithandkraus.com.

Lawrence Harbison

BLOOD AT THE ROOT
Dominique Morisseau

Dramatic
Asha, late teens, African-American

*In this direct address to the audience, Asha talks about
her anger issues and what it means to be Black.*

ASHA

People don't know this 'bout me but I used to have a lotta
anger. You might not think it by lookin' at me, but I could
really throw down. When I was nine, my Mama and Daddy
got a divorce. Was fightin' and fightin' all the time and couldn't
never get on the same page. So they split. I went to stay with
Mama in Florida for a while 'fore she moved here to Louisiana.
But when I was 'bout ten, I started gettin' in all this trouble at
school. Fights and everything. Just mad all the time and didn't
know why. So my Mama sent me over to live with Daddy in
Georgia for a coupla years. He had himself a new wife and
everythang. Livin' good in Hotlanta with a new house and all
that. Wife was a black woman. Her name Sharon and she was
cool as hell. I liked her out the gate, and that's sayin' a whole
lot cuz I ain't like nobody out the gate who be datin' my Daddy. But she was somethin' special. Treated me like a daughter.
Didn't try to replace my mama or nothin' like that, or even act
like she could. I think that's what I liked about her. She was
just real easy with me. Ain't had her own kids, but had a bunch
of nieces and nephews and she told 'em to call me cousin. So
they did. Used to hang with 'em whenever it be a family get
together. They say "whaddup cuz" like that, and I remember
feelin' for the first time like I belonged somewhere. Like finally I ain't need to fight no more cuz I was in company that felt
like home. And I stopped be so angry all the time. Angry at
Mama and Daddy. Angry at myself, even. Angry at the world.

(beat) After while, Mama called fo' me to come move with her here. I was like twelve. But I wunn't the same no mo'. Ain't feel as comfortable back here. Not til' I started hangin' out again with... —— (beat) They used to call me "black by association." Alla my friends and play cousins in Hotlanta. But here they just call me "fake" or "wannabe" or "actin' black." But you know what I thank? If actin' black mean bein' like Sharon... Mean findin' family and love in places you wunn't expectin'. If it mean not bein' angry unless you got good rea-son.... Then maybe we should all be "actin' black" mo' often. That's all I got to say 'bout that.

For information on this author,
click on the WRITERS tab at www.smithandkraus.com.

BLOODLETTING
Boni B. Alvarez

Dramatic
Leelee Flores.19, Filipino

Leelee is a young aswang, a Filipino witch. She speaks to Farrah Legazpi, a Filipino-American woman visiting the Philippines to spread her late father's ashes. Farrah has just discovered that she is also an aswang. Leelee describes an aswang's greatest pleasure: feasting on fetuses.

LEELEE

Some nights, your teeth grow longer and sharper. The moon tells you where to go, where the expecting mothers are sleeping. Your blood cools as you lower your teeth into the belly button. You take a deep breath and you suck. You drain out the juices... Imagine you are so hungry, Manang. As if you have not eaten in months. Your tongue like salted fish, but you cannot find a way to swallow it. You cannot hold your body up, your mind grows too weak. It is only the juices that can save you. You drink so carefully. You do not waste, like kissing the belly - nothing dribbling from the sides of your mouth. The little little body, your savior. Made only for you. Every piece increases your strength. Your heart pumps strong. Your blood moving inside like a healthy river. And then the cord. You bite. Seems so tough, hard plastic, with no flavor. But you must chew. Use your teeth, continue chewing and chewing. Your tongue gains back feeling, restoring your *laway*. And the cord, it burst. The warmest, most golden pineapple, freshly candied cashews, steaming *arroz caldo*, the flavors so powerful, filling you with energy, with life.

For information on this author,
click on the WRITERS tab at www.smithandkraus.com.

CHASING THE STORM
Sandra A. Daley-Sharif

Dramatic:
Aquah, 20s, African-American

Aquah, against her better judgement returns with young Deniel to bury his family, who were all killed by RoboCops. She knows they are soon to return...

AQUAH

Deniel! I came out here to be by myself. To start over new. Start a new life. The future of my family depends on it. I'm on my way to find something. Your mother's right. God has fucking been hard. And, that's putting it mildly. Not just to her. To my mother. This devining, pulled by water, and the visions drove my mother crazy. Drove my father off. That's another story. I waited for him. Just waited... And finally, I got sick of waiting for him to come back. Nobody stays around crazy talk for too long... so it was just me and her. You don't get it! I had to leave her! She knew it! Your mother knew it! It's all here.
(She refers to the journal.)
I'm sure her story is like mine. Like my mother's. I have to! I have to move. I am being pulled from my gut. From my heart. OR, I'm going to die. Die with her. I feel it. So, yes. She sent me off. Because I'm different. Never been attached to much. Never needed much. So, I left her there, surrounded by all her things. Things she couldn't bear to part with anyway. Her dresses. Her books. I kept dreaming. I see it in my dreams. And in her dreams. I see her dreams. I said to her, "Come with me!" I didn't want to come out here alone. Like she didn't birth me. Like that doesn't count for anything. But she was scared. Scared. At least that's what she showed me. Too scared to live. That's what she showed me. She said it herself. "Go on. You suppose to do this." By myself!? "You suppose to do

this!" That's been the story. That's all she knows. Her books and dresses. I swear, I wouldn't of left her. I swear.

CLICK
Jacqueline Goldfinger

Dramatic
Fresh, 17

Fresh is a college freshman describing her experience of being drugged and raped at a frat party to a friend about a year after it happened.

FRESH

In the far distance, Seemingly in the far distance, I hear the click of camera phones and a Shakira ringtone. Click, Click Click. Click click click click click. The sounds come closer, become clearer, And then I start to feel, Pressure, Clawing through a dense mist of booze and pills, Then the monstrous pounding that I hear inside of me before I feel it. At first, it sounds, like Clickclickclickclickclickclickclickclickclickclic kclickclickclickclickclickclick But then it melts into, searing pain, and sounds bleed into one another, Chants and clicks and spilled beer and slaps on my ass. The pain, ripping, I know I'm dead. I'm dying. I just wish I'd die faster. Party music. Vomit. Slaps base line laughter. Chants. Moans of pain, coming from inside of me, living inside of me, only to die inside me? Moans smeared across one another. My head out a window or maybe in a toilet. There was a toilet and a tub. But the window was first. The sounds of praying to die. I could have been stretched across a rock in the Congo, my girlfriend watching as my brother corrects me. Or shoved over the backseat of a bus in India being sodomized with a broom handle. Or stood up against the shattered wall of our stone house in Syria, a cum catcher for an entire squadron of child soldiers. But I'm not. I'm here. In America. Where student safety is priority one. And when they are done, they just walk away. Like anywhere else in the world. 12 Except now, it's seen. Sometimes you want to be invisible, and they won't even allow you that. Click click. We're here. Click click. We're done. Click click. I hate that fucking sound.

COWBIRD
Julie Marie Myatt

Dramatic
Lorna, 40s

Lorna is speaking to her boyfriend, Bert. She is trying to reconcile her past, and to defend herself now that three of the children she gave up for adoption, for which she was paid handsomely by the parents, have landed at her door, wanting to meet her. She has had twelve babies in her lifetime, and given them all up for adoption, often to support herself. Bert is trying to help her see things from the perspective of the children, who are now young adults, and why they might want to know who she is.

LORNA

To good families! To good families. To lonely fucking couples! People foaming at the mouth for babies! Those kids are lucky! And they come back here looking me in the eye like I did something wrong! They want to know why...they want me to sit them down on my knee and rub their foreheads and tell them I did what was best for all of us and then they want me to touch their cheeks and tell them I love them and that never a day has gone by that I haven't thought of them...and then they want me to take them into my arms and cry and tell them how much I've missed them and how sorry I am, they want me to smooth down their hair, tell them what fine men they've become...but I won't do it! I won't. That's not what I'm here for. No sir. That's not my part. I gave birth for Christ's sake—-I may have given birth to those kids but that's it. They are lucky! Don't they see that! One day in a doctor's office and they could have been air. Scraped clean. Could have been tossed into a bucket of red blood clots. The end. They could have been no-

---

things. But no. No. That's not what happened. Sacrifices were made. A body was stretched and pulled out of shape just to house them. Screams of pain were shouted through clinched, gnashed teeth just to bring them forth. But they are here, aren't they? They are here. Because of me. You don't bother the stork once it's done. No sir. You don't come asking for more. You don't come till up the cabbage patch. They already got all they are getting from me. That's it. Breath of life is all you get from me, kids.

COWBIRD
Julie Marie Myatt

Dramatic
Lorna, 40s

Lorna is speaking to her boyfriend, Bert. She is trying to reconcile her past, and to defend herself now that three of the children she gave up for adoption, for which she was paid handsomely by the parents, have landed at her door, wanting to meet her. She has had twelve babies in her lifetime, and given them all up for adoption, often to support herself. Bert is trying to help her see things from the perspective of the children, who are now young adults, and why they might want to know who she is.

LORNA

My life. That's not much to ask. They want pieces of it. They want reasons and stories and names and pictures and faces and skin colors and eye colors and freckles and birth marks and memories and explanations I didn't save for them. I didn't even keep them for myself. That's not what I do. I don't hold on to things like that, I just run through them. I like it that way. I like the way I do things and the money all those couples gave me let me do it. It's not that complicated. They wanted something they couldn't make themselves, and I gave it to them. Like, like a shoe smith. I gave them the right fit...but now all these goddamn shoes are walking back here asking me what type of leather I used and why didn't I wear them myself and which goddamn cow forked over the skin. I want my privacy back. I want my body back. They look at it and they steal something from me and then something starts to hurt. I feel this pull in my stomach and my tits, look at my tits...but my mind...my mind feels the same way I did when I turned over in that delivery room with every one of them...it feels fifteen miles down the road with a cigarette in my hand and two year's rent in my pocket and they aren't getting near it. They can take my tits with them, suck away...I won't be using them...but they are not getting the goods, you see...they're not getting the girl with it... this is what keeps Lorna Cotes alive and free and they aren't getting it.

CRY IT OUT
Molly Smith Metzler

Dramatic
Jessie, 30s

Jessie, a new mother, has bonded with another young mother, Lina, to whom she is speaking. Jessie is/was a lawyer but she would rather be a stay-at-home mom.

JESSIE

I....don't think I'm going back. I mean, I'm supposed to. On May 15th. And I took my suits to the dry cleaners and reserved a spot for Allie at North Shore. My mother-in-law knew someone who knew someone. And paid for it. I know. We're very lucky. *(beat)* But anyway I hope she *doesn't* go there because as I was saying, ever since we almost lost Allie, I kind of... *don't* care about protecting the legal interests of a bunch of corporations anymore. *(beat)* Not that I've figured out how to tell Nate all this. He's a planner— his business brain, I think— and he has us on a ten year plan that depends on us being double-income. He comes from a home where his mother didn't really *raise* the four children— there was a Baby Nurse, then there was a Nanny, then there was a Family Assistant, so he's not going to understand, why I would want to do it myself. *(beat)* He actually... he actually tried to take me to Tulum Mexico a few weeks ago. He came in all gallant, with a lingerie box, saying Pack Your Bags Baby, it's time for us to Get Back to Our Marriage. And he looked at me like I had two heads when I said *there is no way I'm leaving this baby.* But that's what he knows. His father did that for his Mom after each baby— a month in Provence while the baby nurse settled things. So he doesn't understand. *(beat)* It's just been hard though. He told me this morning he misses me. But not in the *I don't see you, I miss you so much* way— in that *other* way. The way that's kind of an insult, you know? The "I miss you *because you've changed*— I miss the *old* you" way. And I just wanted to punch him in his face and say I *haven't* changed, THIS *IS* ME! THIS *IS* ME, THIS HAS ALWAYS BEEN ME, THIS WILL ALWAYS BE ME— AND YOU CAN'T TAKE ME TO TULUM MEXICO! I DON'T WANT TO GO HAVE SEX IN TULUM MEXICO WHEN WE ALMOST LOST OUR BABY, YOU MOTHER-FUCKER!!!!! *(beat) (upset)* Sorry. My doctor thinks I should go on antidepressants.

For information on this author,
click on the WRITERS tab at www.smithandkraus.com.

CRY IT OUT
Molly Smith Metzler

Dramatic
Adrienne, mid-late 30s

Adrienne's husband Mitchell is very concerned about what he perceives to be a lack of interest in their newborn daughter. He has tried to get her to join a Mommy group consisting of 2 other new mothers in the neighborhood, to no avail. One of them, Jessie, has suggested to Mitchell that maybe his wife is suffering from postpartum depression. Adrienne has come over to egg Jessie's house and to lay into her.

ADRIENNE

Did you tell my husband I have postpartum depression? (Beat.) That's what he said in therapy just now — *and I don't have postpartum depression.* Not that that's your business, but I don't. I have a psychiatrist who has *not* stamped my file with postpartum. In fact, there aren't any stamps on my file. Of any kind. I don't even need to take a *goddamn multi-vitamin. Don't you know what depression looks like?* My roommate at Brown had depression. She binge ate pizzas and cut herself. This isn't depression, you moron. This is rage. What I have *is rage.* I am Enraged. It's 2017, and I make as much money as my husband and I work as hard as my husband and I'm as ambitious as my husband and I daresay those are the very traits he found so *goddamn irresistible* about me that he proposed on our third date. And we have spent fourteen years working side by side, our heads in our lap-tops side by side, working from morning to dusk side by side.... so I'm having *a little bit of trouble understanding why—* in the name of God— there's something *wrong with me* that I don't suddenly want to close that laptop.

That I don't want to sit around here in sweatpants singing Moo-sha Boom or whatever the fuck, staring at some baby monitor like it's a lava lamp. *Why does that mean there's something wrong with me?* You diagnosed me to my husband with the Big-Term terms, why don't you tell me. With your little Baby Sling and your little dainty Pearl Necklace and your goddamn Pinterest Page. (Yes, I looked you up. I saw your Pinterest Page with its goddamn doilie pinecone craft shits on there.) *My husband thinks you are God's Gift to Maternity.* He watches you out that telescope like some stalker and then complains to our therapist that *I've ruined his life* by not being more like you. That I'm some Cruel Woman just like his mother, because I'm not doing back-flips to wipe baby ass. *Like some alien has taken over his wife's body.* And I just want to punch him in the face because guess what, Mitchell, *an alien did take over my body.* I had to have four fucking IVF miscarriages to get this baby. And if that wasn't enough, when she finally did show up, the goddamn c-section caused the cartilage in my wrist to develop some rare fucking tendon thing called DeQuervains' syndrome— also known as "Mommy Thumb"— so now I'm in my studio like a *gimp*, unable to hold my flame straight, and I *can't* hold her. I'm sure he didn't tell you that, did he. I can't hold her. I cannot physically bend my thumb more than 45 degrees. But that doesn't mean I don't touch her. *Of course I touch her.* I take breaks and come up and sing to her, and talk to her, and show her what mommy's working on but I don't do that when Mitchell's home because *Mitchell's home.* And the Old Mitchell *would've understood that*, by the way. The Old Mitchell would've understood that I am trying to manage *the single most demanding professional time* of my life. It's Bar-ney's. If this was Mitchell? If this was Mitchell's deal he was closing, no one would look twice at this. They'd just say— *Oh, he's working, what a big time this is for him, good thing there's an excellent nanny, good thing he'll have that baby's whole life to get to know her.* But because it's me, because I dared to go back to my studio, I'm the Antichrist. *Why are you calling me?* Stop calling me. Stop talking to my husband about me. Stop looking at me— *I can feel you looking at me from down here.* Stop sitting with my nanny at story-time. Stop touching my kid. Stop inviting me to things. Stop nursing your baby out here with your tits out in the open like you're a cow at pasture. *Stop doing what you're doing, lady, because you're making it incredibly hard for women like me to do what we need to do and.... I fucking give up, on women like you. (in real agony)* And now my wrist hurts.

For information on this author,
click on the WRITERS tab at www.smithandkraus.com.

DISTRICT MERCHANTS
Aaron Posner

Seriocomic
Nessa, 20s-30s, African-American

Nessa works for Portia. They are genuinely close and there is a bond of love between them, but there is also profound inequality, and the relationship works on Portia's terms. Portia has just said something deeply objectionable to Nessa, and she can't say anything to her mistress, so she turns and speaks to us, the audience, instead.

NESSA

Do you think it's possible to love and hate someone so much at the exact same time? Do you? I mean, I never imagined anyone could tick me off worse than my little sisters, but this white lady just gets on my damn tits! Now, I know, she was born with blinders on… and everyone tells her every day she has perfect vision… so maybe it's not her fault. And maybe trying to get her to see the world from where I stand is like… trying to teach a fish to walk… or a cat to talk, but…but she's sharp as a tack about so many things, it's hard to not to take it personal. She tells me all the time she loves me, and she's "on my side", and I even know those things are true, but my real question is this: What do you think she actually *see* when she looks at me? Does she just think… oh, that Nessa… it must be hard, being her, but… you know… I'm really quite good to her, and I give her my old clothes and things, and she's doing better than so many of her people, so… that's okay, right? I have… *all this*… and she has… *none of that*… and I did nothing to deserve all the things I have, and she did nothing to *not* deserve all the things she *doesn't* have, but that's just… that's just………… *What*? That's what I want to know. That's just *what*? How does she finish that thought in her mind? *Or does that thought never form in her mind?* Is that even possible???

For information on this author,
click on the WRITERS tab at www.smithandkraus.com.

DISTRICT MERCHANTS
Aaron Posner

Seriocomic
Portia, 20s-30s

Portia, a wealthy white woman, is speaking to Benjamin Bassanio, whom she loves. He is actually African-American and passing as white to woo her, but she does not know that.

PORTIA

So, here's the thing... And I probably shouldn't say any of this but I'm just going to say it anyway because I've been thinking it... (and if I don't *say* what I'm thinking I find that I end up just *thinking* what I'm thinking over and over and over again and finally realizing the time to say it was back when I first thought it and by the time I finally do say it either it has grown so big or gotten so blown out of proportion in my mind that I totally regret not saying it back when I thought it, or the moment passed altogether and then the time is no longer right and the world has moved on and the thing I really wanted to say just becomes this regret, this passed moment, this missed opportunity which I so, so, so wish I had taken back when I could have taken it but I didn't so now it's gone and I really, really hate that so I'm just trying these days to just go right on and say what I really want to say when I really want to say it. Right. Well... I like you. I *really* like you. I mean, I REALLY like you, and *that*, to be honest, is scaring the living crap out of me (excuse my language), sometimes literally, though, my stomach is all twisty and churn-y and sometimes I can't quite eat or swallow, even, because I'm thinking about you and your energy and your smell and, I know, I know, I shouldn't be saying any of this, it isn't right or proper or smart or good or something to just go ahead and say out loud all the things you are thinking or feeling or wanting (or wanting to be feeling), no, just kidding, ha ha ha, anyway, the thing is I think you might be *him*, you know what I mean, Him, the one, the guy, the guy I've been waiting for and dreaming about and picturing in some odd way since I was, oh, eight or nine or maybe younger, my prince, my knight, my GUY, but you are just... well, I don't know how to put it into words, but *just the kind of man* I've always dreamed about, somehow, without knowing how, or who, and it's not quite how you look or what you say but somehow something about just Who You Are that somehow seems just entirely, ridiculously, absurdly RIGHT for me, that feels like The Man Who I Am Supposed to Marry, and, great, now I just went ahead and said that right out loud.

For information on this author,
click on the WRITERS tab at www.smithandkraus.com.

EL NOGALAR

Tanya Saracho

Dramatic
Dunia, 20s

*El Nogalar is an adaptation of Chekhov's The Cherry
Orchard, reimagined in present-day Nuevo León in the
Galvan's pecan orchard. Dunia, the Galvan's young
housekeeper, and the only "help" that the family is
still able to afford, practices English with Anita as she
gives her young mistress some advice on men.*

DUNIA

I need a real man. Who wants a *ñoño* like that? Imaginate. We
will start getting into kissing and he will faint and have an at-
tack from excitement. *Asi que lo pusimosde patitas en la calle.*
[So we kicked him to the curb.] Good bye, baby. Men are easy.
There is not one easier animal on the planet than a man. I'm
not being a bad person when I say this. So yes *las feministas*
who like to say progressive things on the morning shows. They
will speak to us about equality and things like this. *Pero no.*
Men are stupid animals. They are smart, but they are stupid
animals. *Esto de lidiar con ellos es facil.* [Dealing with them is
easy.] But only if you have... *moneda con que negociar.* [Cur-
rency to trade.] You have to have... something they want. And
no I'm not talking about sex. That only lasts three minutes and
that's all you got. You lose them after they're done. No, I'm
talking something else. Like to possess. Men like to know they
are masters and owners of you. And you must let them know
that this is so. Even if it is a lie. You only must let them think
that you are something to be won. You make a face at me, but
you profoundly you know it is true. This is what our mothers
and grandmothers teach us from always and we stop listening
because we say we are modern, but they are always correct.

ENFRASCADA
Tanya Sarcho

Comic
Cat, 40

*When a terrible split turns Alicia's world upside down,
she turns to Folk Magic to heal her suffering. Cat, a
conjure woman of the Hoodoo tradition, guides poor
Alicia in her efforts to revive her boyfriend's love for
her through carefully engineered magic.*

CAT

Hhmm... Tell you what. I'm going to do the "Intranquil Spirit"
for you and I'll throw in a "Bitch Be Gone" for that little
tramp. Make that bitch be good and gone forever. That still
won't fix you two when he does come back, but we'll worry
about that when we come to it. For that I will charge you $125
and I like you, so I'm going to give you a spell to do on your
own that will probably help more than most anything. This
spell is older than almost any spell I know. This spell, it's in the
Bible, girl. You ever made a honey jar? Write this down. You
take a jar. Any jar. You put a whole thing of honey in there,
two cinnamon sticks, and some brown sugar. Then you tear off
a piece 28 of brown paper bag write his name on it, then you
put your name in a circle trapping him nine times- His whole
God-given name. Written clockwise. You close it up real tight.
So tight. Then everyday. Now you gotta do this EVERYDAY.
You shake it. You shake that honey jar. You shake it and you
think lovely things. You think about when he used to make
love to you, when he used to rub your feet and tell you nice
things. You think about the times he made your leg shake like
a doggy. Anything that you can feel in your body. Put all you
energy into this honey jar, to sweeten him back to you. (dead
serious, very clear) And no matter what. No matter what, you

NEVER-ever open the jar. Listen very carefully, you open the jar, the whole thing sours. You understand that? While you do that, I'll be working on your "Intranquil" and your "Bitch Be Gone." And no, that's not a necessarily nice spell. But you leave that one to me.

FIRE IN DREAMLAND
Rinne Groff

Dramatic
Kate, 30s

Kate describes a movie that was very meaningful in her life.

KATE

And just like that, the flames zoom across the floor crazy fast; the tar catches fire. And some guy further down shouts, "Fire." And another guy gets on a phone, and he's screaming into the phone: "Fire In Dreamland." Fire in Dreamland. And that's when you see the Animal Tamer in the flesh for the first time. In the midst of all this. There are flames everywhere. Flames. Firemen. Mermaids. Midgets. Panic. Everybody getting the hell out of Dreamland as fast as they can. Everybody except the Animal Tamer. He's pushing past everybody in the wrong direction, into the flames. At first, he seems crazy or confused, but then you get it: He's an Animal Tamer. So where are his animals? Inside the Big Top, all these cages lined up around the perimeter; and each cage filled with totally freaked-out like wolves, bears, leopards, friggin' elephants. And the lions, too. Even the Black Prince is locked in his cage, trapped, smelling the smoke in the air. The Animal Tamer grabs some hapless boys who didn't make it out of the park yet and he's like: Listen, all we have to do is keep the animals from panicking until the Firemen get this disaster under control. And I know how to do that. So he does this incredibly beautiful thing. He organizes it so that they release all the animals at exactly the same time, all of them at once, into the center ring; and, Holy Moly, if they don't start the show! The Animal Tamer gets them all moving in this synchronized, interconnected order, going through their routines: jumping

---

through hoops, and rolling over, and up on their hind legs. It is the greatest performance the world has ever seen. Except no one is there to see it. No one except him and those boys. And us now, I guess; watching it now. Watching it in the movie in your mind.

EVERYTHING IS WONDERFUL
Chelsea Marcantel

Dramatic
Miri, 25

Miri's two brothers, Levi and Joshua, were recently killed when an impaired driver hit their Amish buggy. Miri was excommunicated from the community five years ago, but came back to be with her family after the accident. But even the enormity of this tragedy is not enough to surmount Amish law, and the family keeps Miri at arm's length, like a stranger. In desperation, Miri prays to God for the first time in years.

NOTE: "Dat" = "Dad."

MIRI

God? God – question mark?
(She shakes her head and closes her eyes for a moment, then changes tactics.)
Levi? Joshua? I don't know if I believe in heaven anymore, but I believe you're there. Can I do that? Can I just believe in a heaven for you? A heaven where the fields are already plowed and the cows are already milked and the chores are all already done and worship is already over when you wake up, and all there is left to do is take long walks and tell scary stories and lie in the sunshine after swimmin' in the small lake, like we did on Sunday afternoons. And eat Mama's biscuits and go for buggy rides with Dat, and listen to Ruth sing, quietly, only for the four of us. Can there be a heaven like that? And will you wait for me there? I think I can do better, for the rest of my life, if I can make myself believe you're waiting for me there. Oh, help. Oh. I always thought eventually they'd forgive me

for leavin'. And you'd forgive me for leavin'. And I wouldn't live here again, not ever, but I'd come for Christmas. And I'd see your little dark-haired babies and laugh with your wives. And we'd be a family. And it wouldn't always be "with us or against us," but just, sometimes, like once a year, just "us." But you're both dead. I'm alive, and I'm here … I just thought we had time.

For information on this author,
click on the WRITERS tab at www.smithandkraus.com.

FERNANDO
Steven Haworth

Seriocomic
Teresa, 35-40

Fernando *is set in Spain. Here Teresa, a Spanish art curator and secret painter, is furious with Zach, a visiting American art scholar and her recent lover. He cannot stop obsessing about her great love, the great Fernando de la Cruz, the artist Zach came to Spain to write about, and who abandoned Teresa three years previously. TERESA is painting furiously and cursing at Zach.*

TERESA

No! I am finished with decapitating myself! I am painting someone else! A certain pig from the New World I know! Do not move! I have many sharp objects here! Remain where you are! No! Leave! I do not want you here! You can never love me. Because of him! You can think only of him! Go away! You are interrupting an exorcism! That is what this painting is. I am purging you from my body!

(slashing brushstrokes throughout)

Out, El Satanas! Out! OUT OF MY BODY! STINKING SULPHEROUS AGENT OF HELL!! I cannot believe I let you enter me, stick your polla in me! *Ay dios! Que estupido.* You think you understand him. You think you understand the work. Do you truly imagine you grasp the profundity of his masterpiece when you have never tasted the profound struggle necessary to make anything of value?! A third-rate critic, you congratulate yourself for not being blind! Compared to him you are the shadow of a man reflected in the memory of an idiot child! But He! He brought the formal experimentation to a maniacal height! Every canvas it is a battleground, every brushstroke it is a wound and the wounds they multiply over and over again, to infinity. And this is merely the foundation, the field on which he plays! He is an immortal! He will be an immortal! He offers himself to the fate that governs all profound struggle and we are both at his mercy!! Oh how I have fallen. I look at you and I want to immolate myself! How our standards they decline as our loneliness increases! I should burst into flames from mere disgust!

For information on this author,
click on the WRITERS tab at www.smithandkraus.com.

FLYING LEAP
Anton Dudley

Comic
Aunt Crystal, 40s-50s

Stephen has just told his Aunt Crystal that his girlfriend wants to break up with him. Aunt Crystal is neither surprised nor particularly sober.

AUNT CRYSTAL

Now, Stephen, I'm not trying to slap a label on you, but my husband had a girlfriend and that didn't stop *him* from making backend deals with working men on a Thursday night, if you get my *entendre*? Bet you didn't know I was married. Well, I don't like to talk about it. I sold the ring on eBay and bought new drapes for the breakfast nook. I figured that was worth two decades of sleeping alone in our marital bed on Thursday nights. I should have known. He liked all those big brassy women with the loud voices. We had them all on LP. They were vinyl in those days. Records. None of this MP3-iTune-Download nonsense. No. Back in *my* day you put on a record and hoped it wouldn't skip! It was the danger made us feel alive. Everything's so easy nowadays. Yes. In my day men never came out of the closet. You just had to guess! Even then, when you confronted them with it, they would take a pistol to their skull or at least divorce you and run off to Argentina. Either way you got the house without too much fuss. But I guess what I'm saying is you never really knew the truth. Everything's so blatant nowadays; you know, I think it's possible to know too much? In my day we were content to *not* get it. We just made do with the mystery. That was what made us feel alive, knowing it was all *unknowable* and yet somehow it just continued on. Nowadays we're so about getting to the bottom of things 'you need an anti-depressant just to walk across the room! No, don't respond. I'm not the best listener, Stephen, no; my philosophy is "Ears are meant for earrings and that's all she wrote." Often times, I think lips are meant for lipstick and that's all she wrote, but my therapist tells me I should talk more. If I don't, things'll fester. I wish the space between my toes could talk, there's a whole lot festering down there. Still. I like you, Stephen, and I hope that whether or not you stay with your girlfriend, you'll still find pleasure in the arms of a man. Lord knows I never did – and your mother? Certainly did not. But *someone* in this family should. And with things being what they are these days, politically and all - with these new sexual identities being created every day - why shouldn't it be *you*? You've got the most up to date plumbing and who cares what you are and who you do it with and when and how and why… who wants to know any of that?! All I want to know is… could one of us be happy with another? Just once? For just a moment? Ugh! I hate it when the ice melts and then your cognac isn't cognac, but a spritzer… without the bubbles. Ain't *that* just a metaphor, huh? No bubbles.

HAPPY BIRTHDAY, MOM
Meghan Gambling

Seriocomic
Sarah
Late twenties-early thirties

Olivia has flown home to surprise her mother for her 55th birthday only to find Evelyn, clad in leather, waiting for a younger man she met on Craigslist to come over for sex. Things get more awkward when son, Tim, and his girlfriend, Sarah, show up unannounced with their own ideas of how to celebrate Evelyn's birthday.

SARAH

Well, while we're all being honest, this is the perhaps the most startling excursion to a "boyfriend's" house that I've ever had to endure. From the five hour plane ride, to the four cups of coffee— nervous I'd make a bad impression — I see now that's a bit of a *non issue* — to the fact that I've held that balloon since 5:30 am eastern standard time because it didn't qualify as a "checked baggage item" due to its propensity for popping. Then there's the not so earth shattering revelation that my boyfriend was still dating his ex until one week ago, whose name conveniently rhymes with mine, and thus far, his entire family thinks I'm someone else. Which brings me here, to a living room consisting of you, the birthday girl, my cheating boyfriend, an escort of sorts, and my favorite stripper. So no, Evelyn, I'm not having a particularly good time. But it was really nice to meet you. I do wish you and young Thorn here, all the best.
(to Tim)
Honey? Are we ready? I think so.

For information on this author,
click on the WRITERS tab at www.smithandkraus.com.

HIPPOPOTAMUS
Libby Emmons

Comic
Glory, 40s, African-American

*Glory is a mom and an artist in her 40's. As she sits on
a bench, watching her children play in a playground,
she addresses the audience.*

GLORY

I like ice cream better than sex. So kill me. I mean yeah, I'd like
to be skinny, but I like ice cream. I don't like pharmaceuticals,
or things designed to make me feel better, I like ice cream. My
partner says maybe I should lay off the ice cream. I say, I don't
drink, I don't screw around, I don't do drugs, so shoot me I like a
little ice cream at the end of the day. I mean Jesus God, y'know?
I'm supposed to cool it on the ice cream? My one small pleasure? How much do I have to give up? I tried not keeping my
favorite flavors in the house, just not bringing home the chocolate peanut butter swirl that calls out to me in the night. "Glory,
come eat me, come stick your tongue into all my swirly swirls!"
But then I just ended up eating the ice cream faster, to get rid of
the shitty flavor so I'd have an excuse to go buy the kind I like.
I'm home with these kids all day, and when they're at school
I'm running around getting the laundry, the groceries, keeping
the place clean, doctors appointments, teacher meetings. All that
bullshit I did not want to do, the shit my mother always did.
Plan a whole week around getting a few hours of professional
indulgence. Why do you think I'm in it for a half pint a day? And
that's even down from when the babies were born, I used to eat
much more than that, with whipped cream, too.

For information on this author,
click on the WRITERS tab at www.smithandkraus.com.

THE HOMELESS SECRETARY
Gerry Sheridan

Comic
Pat, 25 and up

Pat is at work speaking on the phone. She is desperate and hoping to finish the call before her boss comes out of his office again.

PAT

Hello? Hello is this Mrs. Mathews? Hi, this is Pat Patterson. Patricia. Yeah. Yes. That's what I'm calling about. You know, I really think you should give me a break this one time. I can't believe one transgression and I'm like cut off. Someone once said, "The quality of mercy is not strained," - well I think it is at American Express. Isn't a person allowed to make a mistake? Can't you give me a little more time? Look, what happened was, I wrote a check for three thousand dollars to American Express, but I put it in the wrong envelope and mailed it to Sprint instead. Then I went online to order a new ID tag for my dog, and somehow I got my zip code in the little box that says how many tags you want, so instead of ordering one, I accidentally ordered eleven thousand two hundred and one. That's my zip code: 11201. And I used my debit card, so it completely wiped out my account. So now even though I want to, I can't send you a check for three thousand dollars until the dispute is settled. Doesn't anyone even look at these things? Couldn't someone have said, "Gee, this looks a little funny, who would need eleven thousand two hundred and one gold-toned dog tags with the name Mitzi on them and the same address?" Can you believe it? I hit confirm and my entire life is in a shambles. At $2.95 a piece those tags cost over thirty three thousand dollars plus shipping and handling. So, I have every intention of paying you and I think that should count for something. I'll get paid a week from Tuesday and I can send you something then. I even had to stop my company from doing direct deposit because I was afraid every penny was going to be sucked up by that stupid dog tag company. You know, I think when the moon goes out of its present void state that things will get better. I don't even have my ATM card right now because I accidentally left it in this cosmetics store I just had to go into because they have products from all over the world, Douglas Cosmetics. I got some really good bath products there, you should try it. So, Mrs. Mathews, please don't cut me off. Think about it. I make one mistake and immediately the trappings of civilization start to fall away. My cell phone is turned off, I have no credit card, I had to walk to work because I couldn't buy a Metro Card, my gym membership is on hold because they charge my credit card, and I have no money for food. So if you don't help me out I will starve to death Mrs. Mathews. I am, I am on a total economy kick now, so I will get caught up. This was really weird – someone gave me this book on Zen and I opened it at random and read "Life is suffering. Suffering is caused by selfish craving. Selfish craving can be overcome!" It was like some sort of message for me and I knew right then that I could stop shopping and I haven't bought a thing. I have bought nothing at all, it's amazing. So, please, Mrs. Mathews, think about the human side to all these numbers you see, you know? There must be a way, some way to keep my card afloat, huh? Mrs. Mathews? Hello? Hello? Mrs. Mathews? Hello? Oh my God! She hung up!

For information on this author,
click on the WRITERS tab at www.smithandkraus.com.

HOW TO TRANSCEND A HAPPY MARRIAGE
Sarah Ruhl

Dramatic
George (Georgia), late 40s

*George and a new friend named Deborah (nickname,
Pip) have gone hunting without licenses and they have
been arrested. As they sit in jail, George gets to talking
about what motherhood has become in our culture.*

GEORGE

I bet mothers don't hate themselves in *Sweden.* We live in a
child-hating society that pretends to love children by photo-
graphing the babies of English royalty. But actually, they want
us behind closed doors, out of the way, alone. We don't know
how to feed our children, how to put them to sleep, how to
bury our dead. I mean what are you going to pass on to your
children, your *individuality?* You make yourself irreplaceable
and then you die. We're supposed to make these humans and
replicate something but there is nothing to replicate, nothing
which seems obvious and valuable to teach, I mean, how to
be an *American* are we going to fucking teach them *that?* I
mean the counter culture, what the hell is that, if we don't have
a culture to be counter to—we just work and sleep and order more crap from Amazon. So because you can't give your
children *wisdom,* from the *ages,* you say, honey, do you want
this crap, or this crap? And they're like: I want *this particular
piece of crap.* Other countries have children, we have little relentless live-in *customers*—and we are their fucking patron
saints. Culture is automatically knowing three things to cook
that your mother taught you to cook. Culture is knowing how
to live and die. Culture is what separates us from the animals.
We want someone to tell us *how to live* because we're so sick
and tired of making it up as we go along. We just want a slight

bit of wisdom passed down through the ages to us, how to make a bowl of soup, how to tie a knot, how to die, etcetera, and *this knowledge is not fucking forthcoming.*

For information on this author,
click on the WRITERS tab at www.smithandkraus.com.

HUNGRY
Kayla Cagan

Comic
Barb, 25-45

Barb explains why she can't attend her weight loss meetings anymore. She preaches like she's giving a sermon.

BARB

Hello, Friends. Newcomers, I'm Barbara, but everyone here calls me No-Carb Barb. I've been a member for about 3 months. I came here today, as I've been coming week after week, hoping to be a contributing member to this fellowship. I've been inspired by you and I've been educated by you and I've watched our meetings grow, especially right after new year's eve, with the resolutions and whatnot, but…and I say this after much thought and consideration, I am simply not one of you. I'm not judging you. I'm happy for you. I'm proud of you. But I'm not you. I have to savor my own flavor. I have tried the tofu, both soft and firm. I have seasoned my air-popped popcorn with the flavorless substitute salt. I have been to the gyms and taken the Zumba classes and walked on the hikes, and I gotta say it, I gotta be the real me: IT. ALL. JUST. SUCKS! Each and every boring step I counted, each and every cup of skim milk I've measured, all of it, down to the last drop of reduced sodium chicken broth, can kiss my spaghetti and meatballs loving bottom!" I understand the sin of wanting more, wanting decadence, wanting without consequence! I see you, my weight watchers. I see you waiting and wanting and waiting and wanting, (she sings like in The Lion King): the ciiiirrcle of liiife! But it's not enough. It's never enough. I get it. When I hear 7 layer dip, I say give me 8! When I hear Death by Chocolate, I say add Angel Food Cake! And if you serve Trés Leches cake, I'm gonna ask for Quatro Leches, mi Amigas! Say goodbye to No-Carb Barb and hello to Barbara Carbonara! Look, I know I'm preaching to the choir here, but I'm tired of being hungry and I'm tired of meetings and I'm tired of counting grams – I don't even know what grams are! Do you? DO ANY OF YOU? I raise my water bottle of zero-calorie seltzer and salute you. I know you're doing your best. We all are. But I'm out of numbers and patience and points. I'm definitely out of points. So, when you're hungry for more, you hit me up. I'll take you out for a fro-yo *(frozen yogurt)* you won't forget. Until then, friends, may the scale be ever in your favor.

HURRICANE; OR: CLAP YOUR HANDS IF YOU REMEMBER TOWER RECORDS

Brooke Berman

Seriocomic
Cricket, twenties

CRICKET

You pack a bag. A little bag for the Littles. A medium-size bag for yourself. You're disappearing. Just for a few days. Going off the grid. You won't need much stuff. A few pair of underwear. An extra T-shirt or two. That pashmina you got that time. At the Silver Lake Farmers Market. From the lady who sells the incense. At first, you imagine you'll take the Littles with you. They love the car. They love their Britax carseats with the Moo-Cow pattern. Then you change your mind. Grandma is nearby. And she doesn't own a TV set or an Ipad. She may give them refined sugar, but she won't corrupt their fragile growing minds. You make a picture book. Just like Attachment Dad. You draw the pictures yourself. Stick figures meant to represent Mama and her little bunnies. The book is called "Mama's Trip" and it's all about how Mama goes away for 2 days but comes back on the third. In the pictures, you can see how Mama misses her babies and thinks of them every day and comes home Sunday night and takes them for gluten-free pizza and they all go home together and back to preschool on Monday morning. This book rhymes. Miss you, kiss you. Gramma, pajama. And so on. Once you drop them off at Grandma's, you get on the freeway. And you go North. You play your Language Immersion CD's and pick up a few useful phrases in Spanish. Or Mandarin. And you miss your little twinkle-twinkle stars, your babies. But you are free. For three days. To dream.

IN SERVICE OF VENUS
Anna Wilcoxen

Comic
Back of House, 31

In Service of Venus *is set in a fictional, surreal restaurant setting that only serves marshmallows from plastic cups. The setting is the kitchen and food prep area of the restaurant (AKA the "back of house"). The Back of House character, who is a 31-year-old woman, is the main protagonist. The action centers around both the Front of House character and the Back of House character struggling to make sense of their love lives as women in their 30s working a low-paying job and immersed in the digital age of dating where one must sell herself in order to even get a date. The play draws connections between the changing economy of the workforce and the economy of finding love. The Front of House character is a more polished, smiley-faced, appeasing, gentle character, and represents the persona we carefully craft for the public in both the workplace and in dating. While the Back of House character is more crass, unapologetic, less put-together, and represents the hidden, more cynical sides of ourselves we attempt to keep at bay. This monologue occurs in the first 10 minutes of the play and is both setting up the character as well as some of the dramatic tension (Will Back of House make up her mind on how she feels about love and relationships? Will she continue to be single or will she find love? etc.) Back of House is speaking to Front of House in this monologue.*

BACK OF HOUSE
You wanna talk about love? Ok, fine, I'll bite. Let me tell ya

some shit about being 30 and single. . . Wait . . . am I 31 now? Damn it, I am. Well, let me tell ya some shit about being 31 and single. It feels like the whole world is just constantly nagging at me like, "Why aren't you married? You know if you plan on having kids you should do that soon." And I'm like, "oh yeah, I'll just take my broke single ass down to the sperm bank and get some dude's jerk-off soup turkey basted into my Easy Bake baby oven. Then, ya know, it's as simple as settin' the timer for 9 months and then ta-da! Now life can truly begin! You know that's not how this shit works!"

And before you say anything about childbirth being a miracle, just keep in mind that this so-called "miracle" happens 4.3 times every second, which is 256 births worldwide per minute, and 368,640 times per day. Yeah, I've done the math. And that's pretty damn common for a "miracle." Look, I just wonder how many times I have to tell people that I don't even want kids or marriage before they believe me. You wanna know what I want? Ya wanna know what I really want right now? I want some fucking cheesecake. I want endless pizza and masturbation parties. I want to watch that one really cute barista fuck a watermelon.I don't know why, I just do. I want to be like an 80-year-old man and be able to fart freely wherever I am and never have to apologize for it. I want people to truly understand the importance of *Ghostbusters*, and how the Stay Puft Marshmallow Man was the best villain of all time because he was a beloved childhood symbol of hope, and it's hard to defeat something you believed in since childhood. That's complexity, man. And speaking of love, I mean, yeah, I do want love. Of course I do. Just, maybe not in the traditional sense. And I want some cheesecake!

INVINCIBLE
Torben Betts

Dramatic
Dawn, late thirties-early forties

Dawn is a knockout. She is married to Alan, who is a something of a shlub, and they live in a rundown area filled with other people on the lower end of the economic scale – all except for Emily and Oliver, well-heeled liberals who have chosen to live in the neighborhood to show solidarity with "real people." Dawn and Alan have been invited over by Emily and Oliver. Here, they are having a private moment, during which Dawn reveals how unhappy she is.

DAWN

I don't want my life to be exactly like this for the next forty years. I feel sad and cut off from life and I'm getting older... On Monday I felt so down. Couldn't face doing anything. Just watched TV. More reports of dead soldiers. I made some calls. It wasn't Sean's regiment. I thought about going into town but didn't want to see anyone. Talk to anyone. Didn't want anyone asking after him. Pitying me. Any more pity from people and I'll die. So I go outside as it's hot and I think I'll get a bit of sun. And I'm on the deckchair, feeling it on me and trying to calm the thoughts in my head but all I can think about is Sean out there and whether he's safe or not and then I start crying and I can't stop and then suddenly he's there, standing there, smiling down at me, asking if I'm alright. I'm seeing *him*! Next door! He's heard me crying and he's come through the gap in the fence and he asks if I want to come over for a drink and a chat and so I do and we come round here and he opens some wine and I say it's only eleven and he says let's live dangerously and so we get a bit drunk and we're talking and he's listening to me, like no-one's ever listened to me before and he makes me laugh a bit and I tell him about Sean and he tells me how much he admires people who are prepared to fight and die for their country and then *I'm* crying and he's holding me and then he's telling me about their son that died one night while they were celebrating selling one of her paintings and before I know it he's telling me I'm the most beautiful woman he's ever seen and he's asking me if he can kiss me and then he's kissing me and then I'm kissing him and I can't stop myself. Something… came over me. Some terrible, unstoppable force and I know it was wrong but I felt more alive than I have done for years and years … You ever wonder why people like him and her, why they send *their* kids off to university to read a few books, pass a few exams, become lawyers, doctors … While *we* send ours away to some desert to be blown to pieces.

KIDNAP ROAD
Catherine Filloux

Dramatic
Woman, 40s

*The Woman is speaking to a male fellow Colombian
prisoner, who is her lover, for some part of her captivity
in the jungle.*

WOMAN

Charles Darwin? You have no idea. Jean Paul Sartre wrote *The
Flies,* based on the Electra myth. Existential. You never would
have imagined you'd get to spend so much *"quality time"* in
the jungle with me! Maybe you're in love with me? I am in
love with you. You're my only reason for being and I have no
reason for being at all, another contradiction. But we can talk
of everything—that's why it's "quality time," right? Remember Rilke? *Letters to a Young Poet?* My boy would listen to
a tape from school, of Catherine Deneuve reading it. Could
anything be more beautiful than his face listening to her calm,
serene voice? This is what I remember of Rilke now: "Even if
you were in jail and robbed of all your senses, you would still
have your childhood, that precious house of memories. Turn
to that. Look for the hidden sensations in your plentiful past
and you will grow stronger, your solitude will blossom and the
noise of others will go away."

(*joking*)

Well, Rilke is a liar, an asshole, a charlatan and a blowhard.
Who wants solitude? I want my family. My 'precious house of
memories' is nothing! I despise Rilke! If I had his book right
now I would burn it!

KIDNAP ROAD
Catherine Filloux

Dramatic
Woman, 40s

The Woman, in Oxford, England, after her release from being held hostage, wrestles with the present and her memories.

WOMAN

It's been years—my watch is still on jungle time, it's strange. But now the feelings I have for it are completely different. I'm a student again. In England. Oxford, PH.D, theology.

I was trying to negotiate with the guerillas before I was kidnapped. For the peace talks to work the guerillas have to be given the chance to participate in the government. We must suspend their jail sentences. It is essential that we make that move now! Land reform, disarmament—the high commander, who gave me this bible, died—he is with God now.

And forgiveness...? I wake up with a gashed face? The machete goes through my forehead like an egg it cracks so fast. They are trying to stitch me up and the blood is pouring out. The guerilla is barely a teenager. In camouflage. His skin so smooth. Sleek.

It would be okay for me to live without a face. I would depend instead, on my soul...?

Eyes, eyeballs are swimming in front of me into nostrils that dissolve into aquiline cheekbones that sag under the weight of a knife that went in too deep, with the neck shot in by an assault rifle. Look, mercenaries are training here in the jungle.

Flesh splatters everywhere so we are running across the forest to try to collect, fingers, ears? Yes ears. If you can just retrieve the appendages for your face to be whole again…

KISS
Guillermo Calderón

Dramatic
Bana, 20s-30s

Bana confesses to Youssif that she has kissed someone else in order to make fun of the melodramatic style the play is criticizing.

BANA

What do you care so much? What do you care about me? You weren't so upset when you were dumping me last night. You said that you were going away forever to work. That you were leaving me to work in Dubai. Yes. But now I think that's just a big, big lie. You lied to my face. You prepared me a cup of tea and you talked all nice and then you hit me with the news that you have to travel? Forever? Go away? Forever? You're not going anywhere. I know. You're staying here. Because there's another woman. I know it. But don't worry. I know you're leaving me but I won't die without you. I won't. But after all these years together I had hoped… Everyone knows that there's a right way to break-up, Youssif. If you want to break someone's heart, first you have to become distant and weird so one knows something is wrong and only then, after a few months of that you can stab the knife. The knife called truth. I cheated on you. I don't love you anymore. That's how you do it. But you can't wake me up in the middle of the night and tell me that you want to leave me because you got a job forever in Dubai. It's heartless. And cruel. And I can't believe that's the real reason you are killing me, because until yesterday I was sure you were in love with me. I saw it in your eyes. Which means that I, that I don't know what love is anymore. I'm broken. You damaged me forever. But it's not only my bleeding heart that hurts, it's also my eyes. Now I'm blind. Now I can't see love and beauty. My body hurts. My legs. Breathing hurts. I would love to just go to the hospital. Walk in, lay down and say… Undress me. Talk to me. Feed me. Inject me. Give me that plastic bag with the tiny drops. Let me have more blue pills. The red pills. The white. The red and white. The little green ones. The red. Let me press the button. Let me ask for morphine. Let me watch my soap opera. I'm in it. I can tell you how it ends. They get married. Take me to the hospital because I'm hollow inside. My organs are gone. My brain is a cauliflower. Why? Because I just saw the true face of simple men.

For information on this author,
click on the WRITERS tab at www.smithandkraus.com.

KITCHEN SINK DRAMA
Andrew Biss

Comic
Joy, 30s-50s

Judgmental and often brutally forthright, Joy doesn't exactly live up to her name, yet somehow her self-possession, style and level-headedness lend her a certain admirable charm. Here she has just arrived – a little later than she would have liked – at the home of her distraught sister who had recently left her a fretful message on her cell phone voicemail. An increasingly rapid-fire delivery would probably serve this monologue well.

JOY

Darling, my apologies, you must forgive me, but it's Wednesday, as you know – the day I have to take Stephen's brats to the park – hideous, I know, but what can you do? And so there I am, sitting on this hideously uncomfortable wooden bench that's covered in lichen and bird shit, being subjected to the most appalling high-pitched squeals and laughter emanating from those pre-pubescent monsters from Stephen's squalid little pre-me marriage, wondering what the hell I'd done to deserve it all, when I attempt – in desperation – to make contact with the outside world and check my messages, and wouldn't you know it…the damned phone's out of juice. So, then I have to drag these two creatures, kicking and screaming needless to say, to the nearest wine bar where I can plug in and recharge – me and the bloody phone – them crying and sobbing the whole three hours, of course – even though I'd bought them more magazines and fizzy drinks than you could possibly imagine – until I finally get a signal, got your hideous message, unloaded the brats back onto Stephen and charged over here as if my life depended on it. So how are you, darling? Well, obviously you're feeling completely hideous – but, I mean, other than that? Is everything all right?

KODACHROME
Adam Szymkowicz

Dramatic
Reneé, 30s-40s

Reneé, a librarian, visits the grave of Suzanne, a recently-deceased photographer.

RENEÉ

Hi. This is weird. Hi. I wanted to . . . I don't know what. I saw Charlie. I went to see Charlie, I mean. Wow. This is hard. Suzanne. I. Well, I guess I came for your blessing? I know we were never what you'd call the best of friends. Not that we—I don't have any animosity. I understood. I wanted good things for you. Better than what happened. I mean that. I'm not bitter. I'm resigned. I have my tea. I have my books. I'm not complaining. I don't want an exciting life. Excitement has never been—But that's not what I came to say. It's been a long time. When I let him go all those years ago. I guess what I'm saying is, I want him back. Which is to say get to know who he has become. But I can't do that if I don't feel like it's okay with you. I've come to you to formally make peace so that he and I—What am I saying? He doesn't want me. He has his own life. His own ways. It can't work. Stuck as we are in our well-worn grooves. And he doesn't need more love. The love you had was enough for life. Wasn't it? I'm sorry to bother you. Please rest. Peacefully. Sorry.

For information on this author,
click on the WRITERS tab at www.smithandkraus.com.

THE LACY PROJECT
Alena Smith

Comic
Giselle, 23

*Giselle, an aspiring female rapper with a hefty trust
fund and a substance abuse problem, rants to her best
friend Lacy about her frustrations with the boys who
are helping her shoot a music video.*

GISELLE

Why are all the boys we know such dicks? All those punk-ass
posers. Telling me I'm crazy. I'm like, you know what? Grow
some tits, get a pussy, get your heart broken, then talk to me
about my behavior. Till then, you don't know. You just don't
know! You know who broke my heart! Brennan! He was in
eighth grade. I was in fifth. All the eighth-grade girls wanted
to kill me because I was only in fifth and I was fucking that
kid. Brennan was the one who taught me to find the edges inside and cut myself on them. He left me full of holes. Maybe
I should email him. Do you have a twenty? I spent mine. On
drugs. And it wasn't easy, trust me. All the boys are at the club.
They're all stressed out about the video. I'm like, Dinos, do
you think I'm gonna shoot this video where I have to wear ice
skates and bend over and let a thousand butterflies go flying
out my as-crack and *not* be on drugs while that's happening?
And he's like, the whole butterflies out the ass crack concept
was yours in the first place. And I'm like, that doesn't have
any impact on my argument. And where the fuck is Sergio?
And nobody wants to talk to me about Sergio so they all start
grunting and moving speakers and testing microphones. And
then Dinos goes, why don't you help instead of acting like a
crackhead? So I'm like, fuck ya'll I'm going to Lacy's. By
the way, Dinos says happy birthday. So do you think I should

email Brennan? I was in love with him! I *wanted* to do it. I remember it perfectly. In that underground tunnel where the light is blue, up against a tank full of water that was supposed to have a seal inside but the seal was missing ... And no, it didn't hurt. I felt awesome. I got so high off my first time with Brennan I haven't matched it since. And let me tell you, I have fucked plenty of eighth-grade guys since Brennan. I'm still fucking eighth-grade guys and I'm twenty-three years old.

For information on this author,
click on the WRITERS tab at www.smithandkraus.com.

THE LACY PROJECT
Alena Smith

Seriocomic
Charlotte, 22

Charlotte has just come home from work at her boring, exhausting day job to find that her roommate, Lacy, who lives off a trust fund and doesn't have to work, has eaten a bowl of cherries that Charlotte was saving for herself as a special treat.

CHARLOTTE

You always do this! You steal the food I buy and then you promise you'll replace it but the fact is you haven't gone grocery shopping *once* in the entire nine months we've lived in this apartment. Do you even know *how* to go grocery shopping? So suddenly it's up to me to stock the fridge for both of us. No, Lacy, it doesn't work that way. I'm not your mother. I'm your roommate. Roommates share responsibilities. Maybe you should try buying some snacks yourself instead of stealing mine! I don't understand what you do all day. Whenever I come home the sink is full of dirty dishes, the floor is never swept and the bathroom is filthy. Is there some kind of deal here I don't know about? Am I supposed to be your babysitter? Your maid? I already have a job, and it's killing me. All day long I sit there, numb, with nothing to puncture the empty sac of time but Microsoft solitaire. And when I win, those fifty-two digital cards go spilling and bouncing all over the screen, like fifty-two slices of my life that have bounced by the present and died, spilled into the past. And then I Google myself, and all I find are swim-team statistics and date of death that refer to other Charlottes. And then I think, I'm not even special. There are other girls like me, other Charlottes, in boring offices all over the planet, Googling themselves and getting the same random array of tragic little factoids. And then I hear the Xerox machine *humping* itself down the hall and I realize – I am a copy. I am a copy in a world of copies, a Xerox world!

For information on this author,
click on the WRITERS tab at www.smithandkraus.com.

LOST AND GUIDED
Irene Kapustina

Dramatic
Rima, 31, Syrian

Rima, an artist-at-heart housewife, has just finished hosting a big family party and is ready to relax for the night. She walks into the living room in the middle of the conversation with Amina, her best friend. The speech is a reaction to Amina's multiple attempts to reason with Rima to help her figure out her marital problems.

RIMA

I'm really embarrassed! *He* makes me feel embarrassed! He makes me feel like everything I do is wrong! And he just sits there, without saying anything. He waits, waits, and then… You know I have my very own view of life. I told you I have my special relationship with God, my special view of life and people. Not like all other women that we know. I hate masks. I know, believe me, I know that I *have* to be honest with all people, and I cannot love them all. Really, really… I mean it's a fact … because I don't own my heart. You know, heart is heart and you can't judge the heart… What *am* I trying to say?… I don't love him. I don't. And I can do nothing about it. I tried. (Beat) You know, it's hard. I know, I know that the worst thing in my personality is my character... And I have a very, very, very, very, very, very stubborn brain. Every time I say to myself, "Rima, don't do this, don't say this, don't act like this," and then I do it! What can I change? He's a good man but I'm not in love with him. And he knows it! He's different from me in almost every single way, in everything! He's so quiet. So quiet. And you know, I have a lot of energy. He is slow, I am fast. He's so, you know, he's good, but when he gets angry, he gets really mad. I'm mad all the time but it's better than to be mad one time and erupt like a volcano. For example, yesterday, I want to go out, he doesn't say anything, "Do you want me to go?" "Do you mind?" "Do whatever you want to do,"... It's just like that all the time. I sent him messages, pictures – no reaction. I don't like that, okay? I just... I just... all my life I dreamt about a father, a new father, you know. Or a friend, because I like, you know, I told you, I love my father and I love my friends. He's neither of them – he's not my friend and he's not my father. He's just my husband. He's just the typical husband. And I don't need that because I need a friend, I need a father.

For information on this author,
click on the WRITERS tab at www.smithandkraus.com.

LOST AND GUIDED
Irene Kapustina

Dramatic
Sami, 30s, Syrian

*Sami, a young, optimistic, and enthusiastic doctor
is talking to his cousin and best friend Imad on the
phone. He's put it on the speaker mode, and moves
about freely while talking. Imad left Syria a few weeks
ago and right after he left the protests started. Imad
saw some protest pictures on Facebook and asked
Sami to explain what it was all about.*

SAMI

So what happened, we started hearing that some people, some
group here, they are protesting. Seriously! It's happening!
Then we started hearing about these stories that a bunch of
kids had been writing on the walls that "Syrian people want
democracy," "Syrian people want freedom," "It's your turn
Bashar to step down," "It's your turn, Syrian regime, to go,"
"We need freedom and democracy," these kind of very simple
terms. And we heard that these kids had been captured and
detained in the security centers in the city. At first, we were
really just surprised, but at the same time we were hoping that
it would continue. So those kids who had been detained they
were never released, and the families went asking for their
kids, then the officer told them, "you don't have no kids with
us, go and get other kids" and when they insisted more, they
told them, "if you don't want to go and get other kids, just
send us your women and you're going to get your kids from
your women." Then the regime was brutal enough to *kill* the
kids and they sent the tortured bodies back to their parents. So
we are now protesting more and more. We want answers. We
want justice. And we will get it, brother! It is such a beautiful

thing, seeing everyone out there asking for justice, demanding answers. We are hundred percent peaceful, not a single bullet coming from us, but we are there! And guess what? The world is talking about us. Oh brother, for the first time I wake up with hope for my life and my country.

For information on this author,
click on the WRITERS tab at www.smithandkraus.com.

LAST GAS
John Cariani

Seriocomic
Cherry-Tracy, 41

Cherry-Tracy Pulcifer, a forest ranger, 40-ish, has stopped by Paradis' Last Convenient Store, a general store in an unorganized township in far northern Maine. She is checking in on Nat the father of her teenage son. She wants to ask Nat a few questions about his involvement in a drunken incident last night. Nat's best friend Guy, a fixture at Paradis' Last Convenient store, is also present. Cherry-Tracy has a lot on her mind—and a lot of questions. But can't quite figure out what questions to ask. So she does what she knows how to do best, and checks to make sure all is well. And that everyone is behaving lawfully.

CHERRY-TRACY

Quiet night. Except—well, got some unfortunate activity goin' on. Fatality on Route 11: Black ice. Dark night. Moose. Massachusetts plates, though. Those jeezless people aren't qualified to be here, in my book. Moose are comin' out from a long winter, and they don't know to look for 'em. Next thing they know, their spiffy little car's goin' right under a moose. Take the top of their vehicle off, and their head right with it. And they never see it comin'. 'Cause it gets dark up here. People from away don't understand that. One of the last places in the country where it gets dark like this. Did you know that? Oh, yeah. Read it in my *National Geographic*. If the Pilgrims landed, say, just a few miles west of here right now, it'd be as dark here at night as it was in 16-whenever-they-landed. True Dark, they call it. *(Beat.)* Funny thing, darkness: It's not there, but you can't see through it. You ever think about that? Only way you

---

can see what's goin' on in it is if you shine a light. But...by the time you shine a light...well, you only see the leftovers of what was goin' on in it. 'Cause it's not dark anymore. Makes you wonder what you're missin' out on. In all the True Dark we got up here. And I don't know what I'm missin›. But it's somethin'. It's somethin'. *(Beat.)* So: You sure nothin' illicit's goin' on in here, you two?

LOOK AT ME (RUFF, RUFF)
C.S. Hanson

Comic
Bianca, 35

Bianca is a headstrong and sexy probation officer. In this monologue, she tries to get her hotshot brother-in-law to pay his bills.

BIANCA

Sit down, asshole, and listen up. Marshall's in trouble. He's getting calls day and night. Creditors demanding money. My husband curls up in a ball every time the phone rings. Like a scared little pussy cat. But I got this much out of him: It's Rusty Shepherd they're after. I tell him to talk to you. He says you don't return his calls. So, I think, huh, we got ourselves a situation here. Wuz up, Rusty? . . . Don't make me handcuff you to the chair. Who are these people? When are you going to pay them off? C'mon. Pay off the fucking creditors, Rusty. . . . I got people coming after me for your money. I will curse in this house until you tell me what's going on. Give it to me straight. . . . You're building a McMansion out in the woods somewhere. You got Marshall driving in and out of the city, doing what he's told, putting up your shack. . . . If there is one hotshot in this city who can pay his bills — Must be something you can do.

MAN & WIFE
Emma Goldman-Sherman

Dramatic
Missy Merriweather, 28

Missy is enormously pregnant (due tomorrow, in June 2017) and she is questioning her pregnancy and the possibility that she ended up stuck in a marriage with a red voter. She is psyching herself up to confront her husband, or scaring herself out of confronting him, by trying to accept the reality and the miracle of the baby, and by trying to stop time, and by acknowledging her fear that will keep her from confronting Ron for the next 25 years.

MISSY
Sometimes I wonder if we aren't awful, if we should do this?! No way to avoid it now. We are awful, the whole world is awful because we all know the President is awful. One man is never merely one man. Even the government acknowledges that because if you call or write or email or anything, if you try to register an opinion, they count you, and one person counts as more than one person. That's how polls work! Or don't work. So it must matter what we do. It has to — but. . . Some of us didn't vote the right way! Should those of us who did vote the right way have to remain with those who voted wrong? those who betrayed — betray is a strong word — betrayed us? If that is the case, how to find out? We want what we want, and we are blessed with this child. Almost here, any time now. Time should be abolished. No Time! Stop the world! Like the surprise of the election: a rear end collision, the screeching of brakes, the shattering of glass, the sidewalks of the city scattered with blue car glass every morning all glittery with broken blue edges, our daily reminder that here in the big

city, we are not truly safe.

For information on this author,
click on the WRITERS tab at www.smithandkraus.com.

MAN & WIFE
Emma Goldman-Sherman

Dramatic
Missy Merriweather, 28

Missy is extremely pregnant (due tomorrow), and is having second thoughts about giving birth in June of 2017. She is ironing beside her husband Ron (on the sofa watching the ball game) and these are her thoughts. In the prior scene, on their wedding day, one year ago, Ron and Missy agreed to keep their thoughts to themselves. So Missy is consumed with thoughts, trying to psych herself up to confront Ron about who he voted for. . . (Even though these are thoughts, they could be spoken to Ron directly, but he is watching the game and refusing to listen.)

When we bought the sofa, when we oohed and aahed over it, this very sofa, the floor model being on sale and the price, we thought it worked for us. One day we'll sit on it together. We'll cuddle. Even though it's red, even though we both used to be red voters from a red state. Here in the city we changed. We got thoughtful, inspired, and nobody here is red. So maybe we shouldn't have bought it. Maybe it's just a reminder that we may not be quite as united as we think we are! I am blue! Blue blue blue! Am I blue? Why is it every ten minutes I want to cry? I'm having a baby! I'll have a terrible baby. A red baby with a red face screaming with rage who will vote for awful people who will turn the tide and give rise to tyranny! Like that salesguy who kept eye-ing us as a predator eyes his prey We sat there, both of us like tire kickers, like we could tell what we wanted in a sofa while that salesperson was laughing at us. Somewhere inside that guy was a running commentary like: he swings and she pitches! Or was he gay? He was probably gay.

So gay people can like sports too, sometimes. Gay people are probably very nice and have good taste. But there we were, the clueless masses performing our roles, about to be man and wife ready to snuggle up and get close. "And this,» he said, «is a sofa full of love!" as if we are deficient, as if he could will us to buy it to fill our holes, to replace what we lack! He could tell we were lacking just by looking at us when I thought we were the very presentation of love! Touching the fabric with open hands, thigh to thigh, about to be married, about to be pregnant, about to be blindsided by the truck of life bearing down on us horns blaring — !

For information on this author,
click on the WRITERS tab at www.smithandkraus.com.

THE MAN WHO LIKED DICK
Andrew Biss

Comic
Felicity, 30s-50s

Having just finished throwing a small soirée for their new neighbors with whom she was less than impressed, Felicity, a rather caustic, imperious woman by nature, is discovered here chiding her husband, Douglas, for inviting them over in the first place. While this monologue might appear more apt for a woman in her mid-30s and upward based on the number of years Felicity's been married, it could quite easily be performed by a woman in her 20s simply by adjusting that number down.

FELICITY

A bore? If it were simply a matter of finding them boring, Douglas, I'd have glided through the evening on autopilot. Without wishing to sound immodest, seventeen years of marriage to you has turned me into something of an Olympian at coping with boredom. But it was all the rest of it. I mean, really... where does one begin? Aside from the fact that they were both as dull as dishwater, they were wearing matching ugly sweaters, their manners were rudimentary at best, his voice had an irritating nasal twang, she obviously believes that less is more when it comes to hair care, their persistent attempts at humour made my throat sore from having to continually employ my professional laugh, he kept picking at something at the base of his scalp that I'd rather not contemplate, she kept pushing her hair back behind her ears as if she were about to be photographed at any second, and when I asked them if they liked the vol-au-vent his eyes glazed over and she looked at me as if I were speaking Swahili. (*Beat.*) I just don't understand why you would've invited people like that into this house. And how can people like that possibly afford to buy a place identical to ours? It makes me feel cheap and underprivileged. (*Beat.*) It's going to take me weeks to alienate them.

MONSTER
Sam Graber

Seriocomic
Nessa, 18

Nessa, a college freshman, has just returned to her dorm room after her first night partying on campus. Nessa's roommate, Brill, won't leave their dorm room, spending all her time hunched before her computer screen. The time is late August 1994, the dawn of the World Wide Web.

NESSA

Since you wouldn't come and since Greg wouldn't come I rolled solo. Started at the Quad just waiting for good times to swerve on by and say hop aboard little freshman! And this big bicep dude also there was all how the Quad was LEAKED and the good times BUMPING at some zesty frat rush, so bicep dude and I bike—oh, did I tell you he had a bike?—yeah, I rode his bike while he jogged beside but I am SO not frat bait and the biceps creeped me so I pedaled ahead, *see ya!*, explored up-campus where next thing I know I'm bong-blasting these Brazilian nacho Dor-jito rumpshakers with sweet boy buzzing, the only one'd talk to me tho' was this gangly spaz wearing this John Stamos-Uncle Jessie's Girl-sweatshirt thing hawking the keg, gave scoop on some underground bar called Hashtag, whatever *that* is, you gotta be *told* about it, you gotta be *tagged* to get in. Damn, my feet are wrecked. Probably cuz I biked myself zippy tornado style off-campus to find The Tag. And believe me when I tell you The Tag WAS ON! Totally the ons. Just a good vibe with upperclassmen, *what I'm saying*, people with *enhanced* good time skills. So I'm barking all kinds'a chatter with this non-Greg Junior Guy I meet at The Tag named Zach, some all-knowing Quantum Physi-sicicist dude, and he's like HEY: WHY. ARE. YOU. HERE. Like that, popping the serious while Toad the Wet Sprocket pumps the air and the dance floor writhes around us. I's like: cartography! He's like: map engineering? I's like work experience with my Dad, map-nerd society for extra, got late accepted 'cuz I suck at tests and my SAT all kind'a sucked, and this is what happened next, for serious, Junior Guy Zach leaned in to me all conspirasationalizing-like and goes: you must visit the restroom. Mmmm-hm! So I crossed The Tag floor all sweat-floor sticky, past red haze lighting all red-haze-lighty and down narrow stairs 'til I'm in The Tag dungeon before *one door* half-off its *one hinge*, and I pass through…and I'm CENTER MAP. Boys and girls doing weird things in stalls and on stalls and behind stalls cuz it was *only* stalls and I'm a little freaked cuz they didn't talk 'bout THIS at orientation, so I saddle to this other girl but she brushes me off, struts to a stall, whips out her thing, and goes standing up. But definitely a woman. But definitely something else going on. It was that moment, you know, *so that moment* that makes it clear: *we all share the same toilet now.* I wish you would've been there. I can't believe you missed it.

(NESSA is passed out.)

For information on this author,
click on the WRITERS tab at www.smithandkraus.com.

NAPOLI, BROOKLYN
Meghan Kennedy

Dramatic
Luda, 40s

Luda came to America from Italy when she was sixteen, where she met her husband Nic, also an Italian immigrant, who came over from Italy as a stowaway when he was also sixteen. Luda talks to an onion she carries around in her pocket, which often becomes prayer. Here, she tells the story of how she met Nic, who has turned into an abusive, angry man given to attacking their daughters, as he has just done at dinner.

LUDA
I was afraid. Of everything. When I met Nic.
I was sixteen and I was standing by the East River, staring at the water thinking—this is not how water should look… when he come over to me and said, you think there are pearls in there? He said, you think if we dive in and get some oysters we could crack them open and find a pearl? I said, you idiot, there are no oysters in there. And what did he do? He climbed over the rail and jumped into the water. He was…without fear… He climbs back over and he puts in my hands an oyster shell. An oyster in the dirty river! The shell was empty. He said, now I know where you come from. Someone had to find you and open your shell and set you free. You are the pearl and I see you and set you free. He was crazy…but he saw that I am a pearl. And do you know what? I am one.

I loved him because he saw me before I did.

Tina has his strength. Vita has his tongue. Francesca has his spirit.

I like this American saying "no problem." Makes forgiving sound very easy.

I've gotten good at it.

You and I, we've known each other a long time.

You do this for me now…you forgive him. You. Because if you don't…if you don't…I'm afraid I will.

THE OTHER GENIUS
Steven Haworth

Seriocomic
Fiona, 30

Fiona is a Psychology 101 professor who is being stalked by a student whom she baby sat when he was six and with whose father she is currently having an affair. She appears before her Psychology 101 class to lecture.

FIONA

Transfiguration! That word crossed my path today. *Transfiguration.* What does it mean? A change of form into a different or more beautiful state. There is also the religious definition: Christ's transfiguration from mere prophet into the luminous son of God as witnessed by Saints Peter, James, and John on Mount Tabor. But for me the word brings to mind perverse sexual obsession. I've been thinking about perverse sexual obsession a lot lately. Probably because I am being stalked by a student. Please please it's fine. There is no danger. Although the student is here today. Oh, stop. Relax. Thanks for your concern. But let us consider the stalker. Why does a man send a vibrator through the mail to a famous model with a note. "Because I love you." Why does John Hinkley, in hopes of impressing Jodi Foster, shoot the president of the United States? And why does my student make his desires so obvious even his father knows his favorite pastime is masturbating while thinking of me? Oh grow up. *Transfiguration.* My student is obsessed with me because he is desperate to become something other than he is. It is not my naked body he truly desires. No! He desires *me* to see *him* as he sees *me*. Were I to see him as he sees me he would be *transfigured*, infused himself by my splendor, and rescued from his abject mediocrity. That's what he wants. And

I say to him now: not a bloody chance! Your thoughts in 900 words. Due on Tuesday. Class dismissed.

For information on this author,
click on the WRITERS tab at www.smithandkraus.com.

OUIJA
Maura Campbell

Comic
Mary, 14

Mary believes she has conjured the Catholic Saint Bernadette on a Ouija board with her older sister, Carolyn. Mary is a drama queen and decides that she must be the reincarnation of this saint as she floats around the house draped in veils.

MARY

Bernadette Sow-bee-russ. Soubirous. Oh my God, I've conjured a saint! This is huge! Fun facts about Bernadette Soubirous, aka Saint Bernadette, aka Marie-Bernarde. "Saint Bernadette was born in Lourdes, France. She was with her sister Marie-Antoinette one day and she saw a vision of a Beautiful Lady. Nobody else could see her so nobody believed. One day, The Beautiful Lady instructed her to dig in the mud until she found a spring of water. Once again, nobody believed her and everybody laughed but she finally found the water in the mud and people came and got healed from the water and now there is a church built on the site. She became a nun and passed away in 1858 at the age of thirty-five." That's tragedy! Saint Bernadette had a tragic life! This is awesome!

(to herself)

Mary dresses in a flowing robe and walks saint-like around the house while being sure to catch glimpses of herself in a mirror every chance she gets. She holds her face at an angle that might invite a kiss from a male movie star. What if I'm the reincarnation of Saint Bernadette?

For information on this author,
click on the WRITERS tab at www.smithandkraus.com.

THE PARISIAN WOMAN
Beau Willimon

Dramatic
Chloe, 40s

Chloe is having lunch with Jeanette, a new friend who is the Chair of the Federal Reserve Bank and who could be extremely helpful in getting her husband Tom nominated for the judgeship he covets. They have been talking about Jeanette's daughter, Rebecca, who aspires to a career in politics but is doing some things which might come back to haunt her someday. Here, Chloe tells Jeanette about a fling she had in Paris when she was Rebecca's age. What she hasn't yet told Jeanette is that she is having an affair with her daughter.

CHLOE

When I was 25, I was living in Paris. I did a semester abroad there in college and fell in love with the place. Back in New York, I found the first French boy I could lure into falling for me and convinced him to take me back to France. I went to NYU. French boys are easy to find. Peek through the window of any café and look for the chain-smoking brooder in the corner. Mine was named Phillipe. Terrible, isn't it? Following the boy. But it was *Paris*…We had a cute little flat in the 5th. Tiny. No furniture except for a bed – but that's all we needed.
    (in reverie)
He was everything. Tall. Thick black hair that I loved to run my fingers through. These light blue eyes that made your thighs shake. He had these three freckles in a triangle on the side of his neck that I just…
    (an intake of air.)
He was everything. Passionate. Brilliant. We got into so many fights. I even loved how he screamed and slammed the door

when he'd storm out. And how we'd make up after.

(laughs again)

That bed got a real work-out. We made love morning, noon, all night long when we weren't fighting. It was fighting the way young people do. Over dumb things. All that unstoppable energy exploding in sex and anger. He wanted to change the world. To write great novels. To leave his mark. I loved how ambitious he was. And I hated it. Because it made me feel small sometimes. And so we argued – about me forgetting to close the window when it rained. Or him always correcting me on my grammar. Big blowouts for hours. And then ... we'd fuck. Gloriously. And all would be well with the world. At least for an hour. Until I left him. The sublime doesn't last. He also cheated on me. The French. Back then, it hurt. How could he love me and also be with these other girls? Over time I began to understand how you could love someone with all your heart and still have other lovers ... Who knows – if I had known then what I know now, maybe I'd still be with Phillipe. He'd have his lovers, and I'd have mine, and we'd have each other.

(laughs)

Tom still teases me about it sometimes. Calls me his "Parisian Woman."

PIPELINE
Dominique Morisseau

Dramatic
Laurie, 50s

Laurie is a teacher at a tough public high school whose face was cut up by the family of a failing student. She has just returned from three weeks leave to have her face reconstructed to find that the sub did exactly no teaching. The administration wants her to take early retirement. She is raving to another teacher in the teacher's lounge.

LAURIE

Fucking fifth period. Humphries is on my ass. English Department head or not - I told him to give me a damn break I only just had my face reconstructed. Asshole. My husband can tell. And my daughter. I freak her out, she says. Everything freaks her out that isn't painted with at least a gazillion ounces of mascara. Or liters. Or however the fuck you measure mascara. She's fucking obsessed with it, that's all I know. I mean, what the hell happened to teenag- hood? I remember dyeing my hair orange and piercing my nose to rage against the status quo. That was a sort of cause, y'know? But now, it's just all mascara and fashion and next top supermodel housewife of blah blah blha —— what the hell are we doing, you know? Are they growing down? And the substitute was an idiot. I asked my kids what'd they do while I was gone. Three weeks while I was gone. You know nobody could give me a straight answer? Then Alejandro finally cracks. Watched The Wire, Season Four - he tells me. Said the sub was trying to show them what not to do. You fucking kidding me? The cute young blonde straight outta teacher's college. Patricia or Patrice or some shit. What the hell are they teaching them over there? The last sub they sent me showed 'em Dangerous Minds. Do they really believe public school is Michelle Pfeiffer and Hillary Swank and corny fucking music and close ups? I'm a white chick who has never had the luxury of winning over a class full of Black and Latino kids. This is war. Got my fucking face cut by the family of a failing student. Fuck them and their lies and the substitutes that show them these dumb ass godforsaken setting us back 300 educational years bullshit flicks. TEACH you assholes! I left you lesson plans for fuck's sake! Fuck them and their retirement. They're not gonna force my hand. Try to move me from 9th grade, to 10th grade, to 12th. I'll outlast 'em all – bastards.

For information on this author,
click on the WRITERS tab at www.smithandkraus.com.

Lawrence Harbison

PIPELINE
Dominique Morisseau

Dramatic
Laurie, 50s

Laurie is a teacher at a tough public high school who takes teaching really seriously. Here, she is ranting to another teacher about the lack of discipline.

LAURIE

I remember when parents would give permission for you to spank their kids in class. You old enough to remember that? I had this one kid, Louie Gaspacho. I remember him real good. You know how some of 'em stay with you for a lifetime. He had kind of a schizophrenia thing going on. Undiagnosed, but I knew. They should let us prescribe the drugs instead of these bogus doctors. I know these kids inside and out. I knew Louie. Another kid I think Ritalin ruined. But his folks listened to that sorry excuse of a counselor, Ms. Esselman- who would recommend a drug to Jesus if she couldn't get him to sit still for five minutes. Never figured maybe it was her tactics and not the kid- but whatever. His folks would never get him tested for his mental health. Couldn't afford the medical bills. Half these damn kids are suffering from mental illness. That's what the real problem is. A classroom can't fix that shit. And neither can Ritalin. But what do they know? Nothing, that's what. I know what these kids need, but who listens to me? Anyway- what the hell was I talking about? (Pause) Louie Gaspacho. He could be a terror if he was really having a day. So one time he threw a book at me. Nearly knocked out the smart little West Indian girl that sat right in front of him. I grabbed his little scrawny ass in the middle of class and gave him three licks to his backside. Never a book thrown again. That kid got almost straight A's that year. They don't give me my credit for that because he got institutionalized a couple years later and pulled out of school, so it's like he never existed. But I had him functioning high- you know? A good old ass whipping can teach a lot.

For information on this author,
click on the WRITERS tab at www.smithandkraus.com.

PIPELINE
Dominique Morisseau

Dramatic
Jasmine, late teens, African-American or Latina

*Jasmine is in her dorm room at the private school she
has been sent to. She has an earpiece in her ear and is
talking to a friend. Her boyfriend Omari, a student at
a tough public school, is planning to drop out and go
somewhere. She plans to go with him.*

JASMINE
Our school is fuckin' fucked. Bitches can't never mind their
own damn business. Gossip whores at every level. It's like-
private school for what? For who? Ain't nothin' you do here
private! My parents are stupid crazy paying all this money
to keep me away from all the kids in my neighborhood cuz
they're so damn spooked I'll get pregnant or shot or some shit
if I go to Public, but I'm like – they must not've ever been in
the staircase here at freakin' Fernbrook cuz for reals… it's all
types of teen fuckery going on and these rich bitches are the
nastiest – straight up. It's like they privilege bought them some
extra freak or somethin', or maybe they ain't never known
what it's like to be desperate so they rather figure that out
through sex or whatever. It's tragic. And I cannot keep myself
in this wasteland of talent. Stuck up girls in my dorm acting
like I'm gonna steal their fabric softener or grab their granny
panties out the laundry cuz I don't have my own or whatever.
Like are you serious? Bitch I may not have your money, but I
have BOTH my mother and father at home workin' their asses
off at two jobs just to have me study up here with the rest of
you cuz they think your privilege will rub off on me by association or some shit. Or maybe they believe in the false God
of this freakin' Fernbrook Academy that somehow it produces

better people and I keep trying to explain to them that someone like me would actually survive better in an environment in which I am COMFORTABLE instead of being the token poor girl of color that everyone thinks is trying to sleep with their pussy ass boyfriend or take their gotdamn cocaine or crystal meth or whatever, meanwhile the worst shit my friends from the block are smokin' is weed. If it wasn't for Mr. Peterson's science class and Omari, I would slit my wrists. That's why I'm goin' after O. He's not leaving me here to rot with these bougie brainwashed brats. I'm followin' my man. You gonna read about this in one of them urban romance novels. It's called ghetto love.

For information on this author,
click on the WRITERS tab at www.smithandkraus.com.

THE PROBLEM OF VERISIMILITUDE
Jeff Tabnick

Seriocomic
Catherine, 40

Catherine is speaking to Josh (40). Catherine had always assumed that the philandering characters in Josh's plays were based on her own marital indiscretions, but she's just discovered that Josh was actually using her husband, whom she'd always thought was faithful, as his model.

CATHERINE

I liked sitting in the dark hearing these men say these things that I was thinking, I liked that those plays were to a certain extent cut up versions of us, all your bad reviews made me indignant. When I saw that first play? I thought, how does Josh *know* that by having an affair I was rebelling against the anxiety that was becoming me? Is he actually a good writer despite the bad reviews? But. Tonight. I'm sitting in the dark. In between you and Michael. And for a minute, the three of us lined up, it feels like that summer, like when we'd go to the movies in the afternoon, both of your smells or seeing all of our lined up knees, something about your denim?, I was for a moment transported back to something full, to a moment that felt singular and heavy and warm and sweet. And yet totally disposable. A moment that had its own smell. That wasn't rushed into other moments. But then on the stage everything feels harsh and cold and the playwright character is you, so the best friend is him, and as this wife character is going through the playwright's old plays and realizing her husband has been cheating, I'm realizing my husband has been cheating. And those characters have been *him*, and I'm aligned with *her*. No I don't like that at all! That feels left out! That feels misunderstood! That feels... stock! But then immediately, how mad can I be at him? But I am mad. And you, I have a right to be mad at you!

THE RECKLESS SEASON
Lauren Ferebee

Dramatic
Lisa, 23

Lisa is speaking to Simon, 22. Six months after Simon's return home Lisa, nine months pregnant, has sought him out for comfort after being menaced by Flynn at a truck stop. Simon, mired in his own emotional pain, is unable to provide the emotional comfort she seeks.

LISA

What am I, invisible? That's a real question, that's a real question right there, like am I invisible? When you look at me is there a person there or is it just empty space? Because you want to talk crazy, sometimes I have to talk myself into believing that I am not a ghost or just some kind of incubator for some creature that will have a better life than mine. I'm sick and I can't sleep and my husband – or recently ex-husband, really – sometimes wakes me up in the middle of the night screaming and I look at him and he is a stranger to me, you get that? Someone I loved is basically dead and his body is now walking around with this other person inside him, it's like he was made of glass inside and the glass got shattered and there is nothing beautiful about him, it's all sharp corners and jagged edges and the kind of pain that just, it just slices right through you. And here I am in the middle of that shit trying to pick my own guts up off the side of the road in my fucking nightmares. Did I tell you that's why I don't sleep, by the way, because I only have one dream and it starts with an explosion and then I wake up and I spring into action. I'm running around except everyone points at me and I look down and see all my fucking insides are blown out and I have to search through this pile of body parts to find my kidneys, my stomach, and my intestines and then I try to stuff them all back inside because all I can think is why am I wasting all this time on myself when I can hear the chorus of screams and there are people dying because I can't keep it together, I mean literally, I can't keep it together I cannot keep my insides inside. But he's fine, my husband is fine, the same way I'm fine and you're fine. For the most part, our guts stay inside us the way they're supposed to. And you know what the punchline to the whole thing is? I went into the Army because I wanted to be a doctor. And now I can't even stand the sight of my own blood in my dreams.

ROAD KILL
Karen JP Howes

Seriocomic
Lana, late 20s to mid-30s

Lana is a professional assassin who doubles as an insurance investigator. She is speaking to a man who she is following secretly for the insurance company. She knows he faked his death so that his family could collect on the policy, and he could start a new life.

LANA

Tell me about it. Jesus, I was thinking about that lady in the bathroom. I bet she used to have a union card for a telemarketing company. That's big now. Working from home with just a telephone and a computer, and you never have to see anyone and they don't have to see you. It works pretty nice for people who are ugly or fat or don't smell good. But people want to have meaning and purpose. So that's maybe when this fat lady gets tired of all the click, click, click of phones hanging up, and she takes a job at some edgy non-profit fighting for capitalism or Jesus or carbon – it doesn't really matter, just something to give her life meaning. People come here out of nowhere, don't they? They come through those doors cause it's the only place around. The only place where they can get coffee, a sandwich, gasoline. And after all the driving they did before they got here and all they got to do after, they start talking. Then they're telling you what they do. You know what I do. It was one of the first things I said to you. I told you I was a consultant. And if you were actually listening, which most people don't do, you would've heard me say that I was a consultant who was an investigator as a cover. You like that thought? Kind of sexy isn't it? You know what's even sexier? I investigate dead people. People who are reported dead but are actually just as alive as you and me. Do you know, for instance, that people are actually hired to kill other people – it's not just in books and movies. It happens for real and they sometimes don't get more than a few thousand dollars. You ever look at someone and try to guess what they do for a living? Some people clean out porta-potties and if you knew that, you might not want to shake their hand. Then there are others who pull gold fillings out of old teeth and melt it down to make jewelry. You might not want to smile when you meet someone in that line of work.

ROAD KILL
Karen JP Howes

Dramatic
Laura, early 30s

LAURA

My panties are 100 percent cotton and I never buy them when they're on sale. Did you tell that to your Mr. Packard – the way I feel about sales? I should have realized that the concept of privacy runs *au contraire* to PR.

(Somewhere during the following and with perfect demure, Laura removes a pair of black panties and replaces them with a white pair.)

Something is either for public attention or it's a dark and nasty secret, which means there's not one single place in your world for underwear and stockings and eyeliner. God forbid they should wind up in a magazine picture. What about shaving cream and talcum powder and deodorant soap? I suppose famous people don't buy any of those personal items. At some point, things aren't just things. A lipstick is not just lipstick. Two cocktail glasses on a table – much more than that. This doesn't have anything to do with me. It's about what we have all come to. It's about what you have done to us – and nearly single handedly, Billy. It's a matter of whether or not something personal is left on a hotel room floor, and if it was noticed by some magazine columnist or not. It's about dead bodies that disappear out of the blue, and babies who aren't allowed to know who their real father is. That's what it is, Billy. Hugh! Hugh-lett. Let- Hugh. We're in the middle of nowhere. There's not even a mile marker on the road out there.

THE ROLE
A.J. Ciccotelli

Comic
Celia, 26

Celia, a movie director. tries to convince Ken's partner Rob that he is the perfect subject for her reality TV show.

CELIA

Well... it started at your audition. You see it was down to the three most interesting subjects... the Yugoslavian with the cane and harmonica and the lesbian bi-polar Republican and you guys. Well ... that special something was you. He told us all about you. You're quite a character, Rob. I can call you Rob, right? We're going to spend a lot of time here. Every night for at least seven to eight months. We'll follow you around... in the kitchen... in the bathroom... on the futon... both of you on the futon. Together. You know what I'm saying? I just need you to sign this release form so we can begin filming. I love this story... absolutely, love it. Ken told us about the time you guys walked through Barney's and you walked out with new evening outfits for both of you. That's when it exploded in my brain... the perfect subjects for my film... two normal men, living normal lives but one has a secret... one is inadequate in his place in the world and the other saves him by stealing for him. Yes... there is more. The fact that you murdered your parents when they ridiculed you about your other little secret... but you weren't convicted because you were a mastermind at covering up the murder from watching *Murder She Wrote*. To be quite honest it was a bit over the top but so are the Kardashians. No... perfect. The ugly truth. We want to put fucking *ugly* on the screen.

SAUGERTIES
Susan Eve Haar

Dramatic
She, late 20s-early30s

She and her boyfriend, an older man, are in Saugerties, New York to scatter her recently-deceased mother's ashes. All her life, she has struggled to differentiate herself from her mother, from whom she was cloned.

SHE

I do love you. I mean it feels like love, but I don't know if it's real. Am I real? The only thing that feels real is pain. It's so hard. I try, I really do, to invent myself every day, to wake up and be myself but I feel her leaking in. In the mirror, I see her walking toward me. I mean, look at me! I've got her body; I got her spatulate fingers. I'm so scared I'm going to die young. So many of us do. I'll never have a chance to do anything, to figure out what my life's about, to really love, to go through the ups and downs, to become a real person. I'm not like other people and I'm not like her. Though sometimes I feel her inhabiting me, like she's inside me. I have flashes of memory that are so vivid it's like I'm living it—like I've lived her life and now there's my life, but it's all jumbled up with hers and I can't tell anybody. It's this terrible secret eating away at me. Sometimes I forget but then it's back — it's in my brain and my blood in my gut this horror like the me who wants vanilla ice cream and hates egg salad—none of this is really me because *there is no me,* it's all her and I can't cut her out or tear her out she's in my cells. God forbade the making of graven images, well who the hell are people to do it? You have to be very clever to hide what you are, even if you don't know what that is.

For information on this author,
click on the WRITERS tab at www.smithandkraus.com.

SAUGERTIES
Susan Eve Haar

Dramatic
She, late 20s – early 30s

*She and her boyfriend, an older man, are in Saugerties,
New York to scatter her recently-deceased mother's
ashes. All her life, she has struggled to differentiate
herself from her mother, from whom she was cloned.*

SHE

What were they thinking? It's a terrible thing to do, to make
someone. Almost a person, not quite human. My mother, she
was so screwed up — and then my dad walked out, he was
a total dick. She never got over it, he broke her heart. Then
it was just the two of us. Maybe the lab people did it for the
money or to fuck up evolution, I don't know. And the parents,
or whatever, nobody thought about us, the clones. They didn't
care what happened to us. God, it's so wrong and complicated,
who gets cloned, the rich or people whose kids die? If you've
got the money can you make more than one? And then what
happens, you have clones for spare parts or to clean the house?
Is it even fair to anybody? To humanity? The earth's collapsing under
all the people. There's going to be protein wars and droughts. This
is my reality, my day- to-day reality and it's like a prison. My body
is a prison and even my spirit, is it mine? I don't know and it's
unbearable. I'm a real live sensate woman with her rationality
and irrationalities. I'm not a robot— I'm a clone! A clone of
my mother!

For information on this author,
click on the WRITERS tab at www.smithandkraus.com.

THE SECRET OF LIFE
David Simpatico

Comic
Carla, 32-42

*Carla, a self-help fitness guru pitches her unique diet
plan, Shit or Get Off the Pot.*

CARLA

Hi. I'm Carla, and I wasn't always like this. Pretty impressive,
I know. But once I was just like you. Two years ago, I weighed
in at 286 pounds and I was content to sit at home eating candy
and watching the soaps and turning the mattress. I was going to
Hell in a handcart. And I was miserable. BUT NO MORE. It's
not impossible if you have the desire, ladies. Desire and love
are all you really need to get started with my new at-home
weight training program, SHIT OR GET OFF THE POT. I
know it is hard. I know it hurts. I have chewed my cud in the
Pastures of Pain ladies, I am no stranger to the scars you are
trying to hide inside your size 23 house-dress. Diets are not designed for love, ladies, they are designed for punishment. You
are bad so you must deny yourself, you must deprive yourself
until you hit that bing! magic pound and then you can relax
and be yourself and you're right one piece of pizza can't hurt
because look how good you are look how much weight you
lost, you have conquered your metabolism, you are finally a
good little girl ok what the hell one more slice before he comes
back from the bathroom he'll never notice because look how
skinny you are look how pretty just one more slice quick hurry
already hurry with the extra cheese and onions and pepperoni
and oh my God the anchovies and all of a sudden the water
starts leaking back into the boat and you don't know why but
here you are going under again and you start bailing out the
bilge but the bilge is you and they were right you are bad you

are not worthy you are fat where is that goddamn pizza! DO
FOR YOU.

For information on this author,
click on the WRITERS tab at www.smithandkraus.com.

SLIPPED
Meghan Gambling

Seriocomic
Wanda, 20s

After drugging her much younger date, reckless Wanda enlists the help of her sister, Carol, to drag him to a hotel room and figure out what to do next.

WANDA

Yes. I chose Randy's bar cause, you know, it's close and near the hotel in case he wanted to come here after! Which wasn't out of the realm of possibility. I mean, Carol, we talked online for like hours, for days, the connection was real. He's from Raleigh, right near where Mom grew up, and he went to Duke, like a really educated guy with a good sense of humor and I was like "wow, this guy gets me." I was so nervous going to the bar cause all my pics online are from that Cancun trip from after Marty graduated high school in '99. I don't think I look that different but I guess I do. He was sitting at a table under this huge fluorescent light, I mean the whole place is dark and he chooses this one spot like, *waiting* to scrutinize me and I saw it — the look pass right over his face, "Nope. No. This isn't what you thought it was. You, Wanda, are not good enough for me." So fast he excused himself to go to the bathroom, and I started to panic you know — like everything leading up to our meeting was just gone, and there I was alone and I just wanted to say, 'It's me, you know, I'm still the same sassy sultry thing I've always been!' I'm sorry I'm not twenty five, but do I deserve to just be overlooked? Not seen? So yeah, I just put a little in his drink and then, we kept talking and he started to loosen up and I was like, OK, perfect, I can tell him, I can say, "Listen, I drugged you, but *just a little,* — so we can stop the small talk and really get to know one another." You know he could *see* me. And I felt guilty but also, I was going to tell him. But he went from zero to sixty so fast and all of a sudden he's just slumped over on the table, and I'm like, 'oh my god', and the waiter came by and gave us a weird look, but I just patted him and said, he's had a long day. Just like I would if he was my actual boyfriend.

For information on this author,
click on the WRITERS tab at www.smithandkraus.com.

SOMEBODY'S DAUGHTER
Chisa Hutchinson

Dramatic
Kate, mid-30s, Asian-American

After rejecting her African-American boyfriend's marriage proposal in maybe the most politically incorrect way possible, Kate— 30's, Asian-American— tries to create an opening for reconciliation by letting him know that he's not the only one who's suffered interracial discomfort.

KATE
(with mounting intensity)
Do you remember that time when you insisted on taking me to the Onyx Lounge and that bartender—that... *Amazonian,* black bartender with the lip-piercing and the boobs that just... just totally threatened the integrity of a very, *very* small tank top and those fucking stiletto fucking boots that have no fucking business on bartender feet, but whatever—do you remember the look she gave me when you turned to me and asked me what I wanted to drink? You were like, "What do you want, babe?" And she looked at me like...like pouring *acid* on me with her eyes, like she was trying to fucking *dissolve* me. And I almost *did.* I almost did dissolve. I wanted to. I never told you, but I wanted to just disappear so bad. And... and it was like that all night. I had all these gorgeous, black women just *staring* at me...some of them were whispering. Loudly. Not that I could hear them over that loud-ass music or anything, I just mean they weren't making any kind of secret out of the fact that they were talking about me. We would pass them and I could feel how much they hated me and how much they wanted you and I knew they were thinking, "Why is he with *her?*" And that made *me* think... every time we passed one of those beautiful,

cocoa-caramel-cinnamon brown women... I thought, "Why isn't he with *her*? Or *her*? Wouldn't *she* make so much more sense?" And just for a brief moment, I um...I wondered if you were thinking it, too. And I wondered why you had brought me there. I wondered if it wasn't your ultimate revenge, if you didn't bring me there to piss some people off yourself. But almost as soon as I thought it... we were on the dance-floor and you held me like...uuuugh!... you held me like you fucking *meant* it.

For information on this author,
click on the WRITERS tab at www.smithandkraus.com.

SOMEBODY'S DAUGHTER
Chisa Hutchinson

Seriocomic
Kate, mid-30's, Asian-American

When a socially awkward student practically begs her for romance advice, 30-something guidance counselor, Kate has to win back cool points after admitting that she met her boyfriend online.

KATE

We met online. Well. It wasn't online dating, per se. The thing is, my youngest brother went and got himself married…and my mother called me up all smug, asking if I was going to bring a date to the wedding, knowing damn well that I wasn't dating anybody. Really what she wanted to know was was I going to publicly confirm all the smack she'd no doubt been talking to all our relatives. About how and why I was *still* single. Well, I had no intention of giving her that satisfaction. I put an ad on Craigslist. I posted a pic so that the guys would know I wasn't a total woofer. Not that that would've made a difference to most of the men who search Craigslist for dates. (beat) You should *never* do that, by the way. Leave Craigslist to the pros. Anyway, I was honest about the whole thing. I said I needed a date for my brother's wedding, one that would shut my mother up, if only for a single night. And Reggie—that's my boyfriend—he was the only one who responded who total-ly got it. He sent a picture of himself with this big, ridiculous, aluminum-foil covered grin—you know how the real gangsta dudes have those grills with all the bling?—and he was doing this, like…

(she poses)

… cheesy hip-hop pose thing… and his message was, "If you really want to shut her up, just let me show her my big, beautiful… smile!" (beat) Yeah. So I brought him. My mother couldn't look me in the eye the whole day. It was awesome.

For information on this author,
click on the WRITERS tab at www.smithandkraus.com.

SOLSTICE PARTY!
Susan Soon He Stanton

Dramatic
Trish, 30s

Trish, around a campfire, holds the spirit stick. She is in the "hot seat," to tell personal /embarrassing stories to her friends until the group allows her to stop.

TRISH

I liked this girl once, Kelly in the 7th grade. I'd even say she was my third love. Jessica Rabbit, Xena, the Warrior Princess, and then Kelly. I invited her over to my house and my mom made us pizza. Kelly ate the pizza I guess because she was nervous? But she shouldn't have because she's lactose intolerant and started farting. She couldn't stop. I started laughing. She cried and went home. At school, I told the entire 7th[th] grade class about Kelly's hilarious farts. Later in the hallway she pulled me aside and told me how she had only eaten the pizza because she liked me, but now she hated me. That was the first time anyone ever told me they liked me, like that. I guess this isn't so much a story about being embarrassed as much as shame, maybe? I don't know.

(Trish tries to hand off the stick. They won't let her.)

Okay-okay-okay. Uh. I was in the military, and I got woken up by someone pounding on my door at 4 am. It was another airman telling me to call my First Sergeant. So I called my First Sergeant, thinking I was in an ass load of trouble. He told me to call my father. I called my father's cell. I asked him, jokingly, "what's up Dad, my supervisor told me to call you and it's 4 AM, who died?" And, apparently, it was my mom, just a few hours before. It didn't seem real. At first I was pretty composed but when I called my First Sergeant back to try and tell him what happened, I just broke down over the line sobbing. And then, when I finished my tour and moved back home, my brother got in a car accident. He needed a new kidney. I was a match, so I gave him my kidney. Cuz I'm the best big sister everrrrr. But for whatever reason, the kidney didn't take...So now, my brother still waiting for a kidney. And postop, I've been having problems with my back. And I've had to go on disability. Then I got really sad. And I didn't do my taxes for three years...And now I owe 20,000 in back taxes, I think. That's not a tragedy, that's preventable. But it's not preventable, because I was too sad to do anything about it... Then I got myself a kitten! The woman down the street had a cat with kittens, but by the time I got there, all that was left was the runt, and I remember being told not to get the runt, because the runt has all sorts of problems. But then I went on a long walk around the block, and on the wall, in thick graffiti letters was the word runt three feet high. So I rushed back, and took the kitten. I wrapped her in a blanket and felt her wriggling and mewing on my chest, and I felt so comforted, I fell asleep. When I woke up, the sun had gone down, and the living room was cold, and I had a stiff, dead kitten on me. She had died and the wriggling was rigor mortis setting in. That was very disturbing to me. And I wondered how again I could be so unlucky. And I realized, it probably didn't say runt. It was probably a c, not an r. *(A moment.)* Okay! I'm going to pass the spirit stick, y'all!

For information on this author,
click on the WRITERS tab at www.smithandkraus.com.

SPACE GIRL
Mora V. Harris

Comic
Arugala, 16 – an alien who looks like a human

Since her arrival on Earth, Arugula has struggled to fit in with the adolescent Humans she has been forced among. Apparently, on this planet, punching people on a regular basis is not socially acceptable. After her first roller derby bout leads to unexpected sexual congress with her uber-cool teammate Bruise, Arugula has a big realization and almost blows her cover.

ARUGULA

Do you ever feel like…like you're this alien being, who just like ended up here on Earth with all these Humans but you don't really belong? And you're always asking yourself, like, "Am I *doing* this, right?" Like you'll be in the audience at a show and you clap because the Humans are clapping, but you're also thinking, "Is this right? Is this how people clap?" And that's like a simple thing. Talking to people is even worse. You never know what to say. You're never ready with your beverage order. You think people think your Dad is weird but you don't know why. You answer machines you're not supposed to answer and people look at you. But then, sometimes, every once in a while, finally, some one thing will click into place. You have this one supercharged burst of understanding that makes like a hundred other little things make sense because you suddenly realize, "Oh. I'm a *lesbian* alien." And like, at least you figured that out.

SPEECHLESS
Greg Kalleres

Dramatic
Clair, 30-32

Clair becomes defensive when her on-again off-again boyfriend thanks for "opening up" last night about her strained relationship with her father. But when he implies that it "might help explain" why she's so guarded with him — she's had enough.

CLAIR

(fed up)

Jesus, David, look: If you wanna know why I cheated on you, just ask me. *(Before he can interrupt —)* No, because I know you have a hard time wrapping your brain around this. Like how can you keep taking me back when all I do is *hurt* you? And I *agree!* It's perplexing. But asking me to "open up" to you so that you can interpret, for yourself, your own…pedestrian psychological justifications for my cruelty… *(Before he can interrupt —)* And I *understand!* You care for me. And it kills you. And the only way you can rationalize taking me *back* is by taking everything *else.* "Tell me *more,* Clair. I wanna know who you are. No, I mean, who you *really* are!" I screwed up. I apologized. I want to be a better person. You asked me to be more open, fine. I'll tell you whatever story you want about my life. But you do not get to "get me" now. Or have some *insight* into why I am the way I am. Because *I* don't have that insight. As disappointing as it is, I might just be a selfish fucked up person because that's just me. *(After he defends himself)* And I don't think it's weird to say that dressing up like a flapper drag queen in your Baramba's attic might help explain why you're such a fucking pussy.

(She immediately regrets this. She considers apologizing. But passes.)

I have to go.

For information on this author,
click on the WRITERS tab at www.smithandkraus.com.

A STEP BEYOND THE RAIN
Merridith Allen

Dramatic
Deirdre, thirties

Deirdre returns temporarily to her hometown to care for her ailing grandfather, and resumes a romantic relationship with her high school boyfriend, Finn. Here, Deirdre tells him that maybe her life will never be what she dreamed it would be, and maybe she should stay.

DEIRDRE

I had an insane idea this morning, Finn. That, you and me, we could…maybe there was a door we never walked through that got opened. Maybe this was what things were supposed to be all along. (Pause) You know what nobody tells you about? After you dream your whole life about doing something, and you do it — at least, you do it the best you can…after you live a dream, after you wake up, even, you go back to sleep, you never dream the same. In fact, maybe you don't dream at all anymore. Maybe you start thinking, the real part of life was never that dream, and it only existed in this place somewhere out there in front of you. Like you think you could reach for it whenever you want to, but really…really it just keeps floating further and further away. And you're confused — I mean, utterly mystified at how it was you ever managed to touch it in the first place. I'm so fuckin' tired of fighting. I think about leaving again, about jumpin' out of another airplane to leap into the unknown, and I'm terrified. Cause out there, what's always the case is, you do it — you jump — there's no way to know if there's gonna be a net or fuckin knives below to catch you.

A STEP BEYOND THE RAIN
Merridith Allen

Dramatic
Deirdre, thirties

After twenty years pursuing a dream, Deirdre returns to her hometown to care for her ailing grandfather. When he passes away, Deirdre is forced to confront the truth about the past and her present, including the relationship with her high school boyfriend, Finn.

DEIRDRE

Wow...that's kinda...wow, that's fucked, Finn, that's really... you want to be part of us *now*? Twenty years ago, you couldn't get away from me fast enough. You wanted to marry me when we were teenagers. Like, real thing marry me, cause you loved me - story-kind-of-loved me, dream-about-kind-of-loved- me. And then all of a sudden, one day, I start tryin' to hold your hand or touch you or whatever, and you pull away, or you look at the ground, and you don't don't talk to me, you don't call me. And then finally, when we did have sex, you would look at me like it hurt you to be with me. But then how you touched me, still, I knew you loved me, so when we were done and you just turned your back ... you know what it feels like to lay in bed, naked, next to your best friend and feel lonely? Feels like you put your hand over the fuckin' grill, turned the flame on high — that's what it feels like. Like thinkin' about touching you again and you get sense memory of, wait, that's going to burn, I better not do that anymore. You made me feel unwanted! All the time, for SO long! You wanted me to have my big shot? Mr. lay-down on-a-fuckin'-cross-for-me, that's what you wanted? Well, look at me now! I never got out of the back room of a bar either, singin' some opening number for somebody. I never got past some bit part in a chorus, some regional show. So actually, if you think about it, mostly, we lived the same fuckin' life, except I kept swimming upstream following this impossible dream of mine, and mostly...mostly, I was alone. And I really don't have much to show for the last twenty years. And yesterday, I lost the *last* person on earth who wanted me!

(She drops to her knees, head in her hands.)

Fuck you, Finn, don't you come near me. You know what? I can't wait till this nightmare's over. Sunday's not comin' fast enough for me! I get to bury everything I dug up comin' back to this town — EVERYTHING! You included. So you go home to your sad little basement apartment, you lay down on your sad little beer stained futon. You fuckin' run it up the flagpole, think about your trashy red heads, and then you stare at the ceiling, the empty space, alone. And don't you feed me any more bullshit about, you picked me, you wanted to be part of the crew, you were protecting me, or anything else!

STATE OF THE ART
Deborah Savadge

Comic
Chloe, 20's

Chloe, the ingénue in a national tour of a play called
State of the Art, *is in competition with the leading
lady, Margot, for good reviews and for the attentions
of the young leading man, Colin.*

CHLOE

Margot, you are not the director. You are not the stage manager.
You are...
(She takes a different tack.)
It's a two-person scene. If the scene is broken, if the scene
needs to be "tweaked" from the way it was on opening night ...
(pulling herself up to her full height)
... when the Bernardsville Weekly called me, "a radiant new
light in Philadelphia's already Milky Way," then I guess you'll
have to admit that you are fifty per cent of the problem. But
you know, it's really so sweet of you to take this time with me:
to want to work with me, to help me improve. It's so great.
I mean that you still have the energy for that kind of thing.
I *reeeally* hope I have that kind of zest when I'm your age.
You've been putting yourself out for the *youuuung* actors in
the company and we really appreciate it. Truly. I think it should
be talked about. You've had a long, *looong* career. And this
could be your last national tour. I mean people can't go on
shlepping all over the country forever, can they? And we
should be celebrating that: "Margot's last appearance in Balti-
more," "Margot takes a final bow in Chicago," "Margot leaves
the stage one final time in Cleveland." *(Pause)* You've been
like a mother to me and to...Colin. I mean, people like you are
an inspiration to the *youuuung* actors who are coming up and

having careers. I think other "senior" actors would rest on their laurels. I told Colin I'd have dinner with him after the show. Maybe we could work on the scene tomorrow. I don't want you to think I don't care, passionately, about the truth of the scene. Oh, look at that! I've chipped a nail. Gotta fix it before Harvey calls "places."

(She exits quickly.)

For information on this author,
click on the WRITERS tab at www.smithandkraus.com.

SUBURBAN NIGHTMARES
Dana Leslie Goldstein

Comic
Karen, 30

Karen, a temp, is interviewing for a full-time job.

KAREN

Yes, I know I'm overqualified. Story of my life. But actually I'm not. Because, I - well, to be honest, you'll appreciate honesty, won't you? It's the sad irony of my young – I'm thirty, I'm not too young – life that I've never actually held a real job. Not because I couldn't, but, well, you've got my resume in front of you. I don't have to tell you what you already know. Do I have to tell you what you already know? Okay. Um. You can see, from what's on the page, that I have obvious artistic potential. That's why I haven't really wanted to get tied down, committed, you know, to one form of employment - until now, that is. Right. Okay, I'm going to be completely straight with you; maybe not completely straight. I am an artist. (pause) That was a joke. Not a funny joke. Obviously. Sorry. You see, I want this job because... I'm about to do something crazy, something everyone tells you not to do. I am about to be honest. I want this job because I need medical insurance. Not that there's anything wrong with me. I just, well, I turned thirty last month. I should probably stop taking chances. Not that I take a lot of chances, generally. I'm very cautious. But not to the point of paralysis, obviously. I mean, a certain amount of risk-taking is essential to any well-lived life. Well-run office. Well-made garbage disposal. Did I tell you that I've always wanted to work for a garbage disposal manufacturer? Really. Since I was a child. I was fascinated by the gnashing monstrous teeth inside the drain. That's why I'd be such an asset to your ... You aren't buying this. Look, obviously my skills are impeccable, cultivated over years of temp work, which is something I don't intend to do forever. No, siree. Not that they haven't treated me well at the temp agency. They have. I'm a regular star among temps. A true find. I am the pièce de résistance of temps! I type ninety words per minute. Ninety! Test me! I dare you! (pulling back) Okay, that was probably over the top. This isn't working out, is it? I'm obviously not ready to commit. Let's just end this interview amicably, shall we? I'll, uh, I'll keep your card, if that's all right, in case I... In case I change.

For information on this author,
click on the WRITERS tab at www.smithandkraus.com.

SWEAT
Lynn Nottage

Dramatic
Tracey, 45-53

Tracey works at a mill in a Rust Belt town in Pennsyl-
vania whose continued operation is precarious. She
is resentful of the raw deal the American worker is
getting, as well as the implosion of her community, as
she tells her fellow denizens of a local bar.

TRACEY

You know how long I been working at the plant? Forget it...
Never mind, it's not important... But, I know the floor as good
as Cynthia. I do. You wanna know the truth, the only reason
I didn't get the job is because Butz tried to fuck me and I
wouldn't let him, and he told everyone in management that
I'm unstable. I'm not unstable. It sucks. And, I betcha they
wanted a minority. I'm not prejudice, but that's how things are
going these days. I got eyes. They get tax breaks or something.
It's a fact. That's how things are going. And I'm not prejudice, I say, you are who you are, you know? I'm cool with
everyone. But, I mean... C'mon... you guys coming over here,
you can get a job faster than ... Well, my family's been here
a long time. Since the 20's, okay? They built the House that
I live in. They built this town. My grandfather was German,
and he could build anything. Cabinets, fine furniture, anything.
He had these amazing hands. Sturdy. Meaty. Real firm. You
couldn't shake his hand without feeling his presence, feeling
his power. And those hands, let me tell you, they were solid,
worker hands, you know, and they really, really knew how to
make things. Beautiful things. I'm not talking about now, how
you got these guys who can patch a hole with spackle and think

they're the shit. My grandfather, was the real thing. A crafts-
man... And I remember when I was a kid, I mean eight or nine,
we'd go downtown to Penn with Opa. To walk and look in
store windows. Downtown was real nice back then. You'd get
dressed up to go shopping. You know, Pomeroy's, Whitner's,
whatever. I felt really special, because he was this big, strap-
ping man and people gave him room. But, what I really loved
was that he'd take me to office buildings, banks... you name it,
and he'd point out the woodwork. And if you got really, really
close he'd show some detail that he'd carved for me. An apple
blossom. Really. That's what I'm talking about. It was back
when if you worked with your hands people respected you for
it. It was a gift. But now, there's nothing on Penn. You go into
the buildings the walls are covered over with sheetrock, the
wood painted gray, or some ungodly color, and it just makes
me sad. It makes me...Whatever.

For information on this author,
click on the WRITERS tab at www.smithandkraus.com.

TAKING BACK HALLOWEEN
Cayenne Douglass

Comic
Witch, 40s

Witch (a corporate businesswoman with a soft and dorky side) is speaking to Black Cat, Jack O'Lantern, and Ghost. Black Cat has just complained that in October, when he get scared, his back involuntarily arches up and his hair stands on end... and he looks like one of the Halloween cut outs. He has said it's embarrassing because he feeds right into the stereotype and it's not in his control. Witch responds to his complaint with a one-upmanship to his experience.

WITCH

Talk about not having any control! It's been a shit show at work! There's a new position that opened up, one that's above mine, and I *assumed* I would be asked if I wanted the job. After all, I'm the top sales person on the team! I brought in 13 million last year! But does that matter? No! Because they'll always see a witch in power as a liability. So, of course, I was passed up, again. Do you know the lengths I have gone to fit in in that office? I've resorted to taking the subway, when my broom would be a hell of a lot faster. I've stopped wearing my pointy hat because I know it makes people feel "uncomfortable". I've had wart removal surgery, dental implants, and custom-made foundation to cover my green skin, cause lord knows Sephora isn't going to cut it. I've even taken cackle reduction class to be more "woman sounding"...whatever *that* means... but do you know what it's like? What it feels like, to have to hide who you are? Every, single, time, something funny is said, I just want to erupt into what's natural, to be who I am, to fully express how I'm feeling, to –

(She lets out an outrageous cackle.)
but, nooooooo, I'm stuck with at the water cooler every, damn, day with-
(giving her version of a subdued laugh)
I mean, if I wanted to, I could turn that company upside down one incantation at a time. I could cast a spell on Bob, or Terry, or Chad, freakin' *Chad!* I could show them whose boss! But no, instead, I've done everything to fit the mold; all because I was under the impression that playing by the rules would get you somewhere.

TANIA IN THE GETAWAY VAN
Susan Bernfield

Dramatic
Diane, 36

*It's 1975 in the San Francisco Bay Area, and Laura's
mom is going back to school. Diane is discovering
liberation, openness, possibility! But that doesn't
mean eleven-year-old Laura has to play along, no
way. She's in the hall closet, pretending to be Patty
Hearst. Fast forward to 2012. Successful Laura looks
like a model product of the women's movement... or is
she just the byproduct of Diane's expectations?*

DIANE

Y'know, I'm finding my assertiveness training really really
helpful. Let me tell you why.
*(Beat. After a long party of suburban drinking, she
has no idea why. A new beat. Okay maybe she does,
or maybe there's just lots else to say.)*
Because we never we girls we girls girls are supposed to be
you know NICE. Nice doesn't say doesn't say what we're
thinking what we want to do what we don't want to do nice
doesn't sleep with boys before we get married it's me who's
friends in college I'm the only one who'll be *friends* with the
one girl who *does* sleep with boys or one boy her boyfriend
nobody else is friends with her but *I* am cause I think that's
dumb can you imagine the other girls don't talk to her because
she? Of course we all have hot pants so we get married 21 and
I'm married I mean I love your dad but that was miserable
really the wedding night so much to-do and it's so hard to do
so uncomfortable so messy we just we laugh we get through
it he helps me did I tell you this he helps me put in a tampon
I mean not *help me* help me no but he stands outside the

bathroom door and shouts out the directions on the box cause before marriage I never use a tampon heaven forbid *that* can take your *virginity* away can you imagine oh my god the 1950s let me tell you thank god they are OVER Then here we are California there's a revolution there's there's free love kids're getting laid getting high I'm sitting home already sitting home with you I mean I love you all but still revolution just 30 miles away dancing in the streets but that's not all far away not far away they're *fighting* something they're *doing* something Poli sci major I loved it next stop Ph.D. I thought but the professor sent me home is that a wedding ring I see he said shouldn't you go home and have babies I'm a fighter too I could be but I had the damn babies cause we all did that's what you did they told you to have em no degree for me home with three babies trying to get with it get groovy home boning up on protest boning up on my Bob Dylan boning up on my Joan Baez I'll show you Tears of Rage lady I tell ya you haven't seen Tears of Tears of Tears of anything till you got three kids at home under the age of three and you were born 10 years too early to screw in the streets

TELL HECTOR I MISS HIM
Paola Lázaro

Dramatic
Isis, 16, Puerto Rican

Isis ran away from her school trip and has come into the neighborhood. She is finally able to say what she's been feeling and hiding from everyone, including herself.

ISIS

Do you like women? I mean you don't have to answer that. At all, actually. I'm sorry. *(quick pause)* I'm saying cause I've been thinking about whether I like women too. And I don't really have anyone to talk to about it. And the other day, it just hit me, cause I was cooking desayuno, right? And- So I'm cooking breakfast. And my parents, they're old. He's basically fucking deaf. So my parents are sitting around watchin the news and shit. And the TV's loud as fuck. And everybody's fucking dying and everybody's getting killed for no reason. And I'm like burning the shit out of the eggs, they don't even look like eggs no more and I remembered: One of the girl's moms. At my all girls catholic school. I remembered this mom that came to pick her girls up at school the day before and I thought as I was killing theses eggs, I thought about the mom and her ass, her ass was so beautiful and she was so beautiful and her body was real and raw and in my head I was like: "Oh yeah, she was pretty. But then I was like: "Nah, she was hot" and then I was like: "Wait! Isis! You can't say that a woman is hot. Cause you're a woman. That's not good. You're a lady" So then I switched back to like: "She's pretty" and then I was like: "Fuck that, nah, she's hot. And I would wanna give her an orgasm" And then now today I saw you and you have completely dislocated any sense of questioning or supposed stability I had in my life. You have flipped that shit around. I saw you and there was no question about it anymore. I like women.

Lawrence Harbison

A TIME FOR EVERYTHING
Martha Patterson

Comic
Olive, 30s

Olive runs an antique shop but, despite never having acted before, is desperately trying to get an audition as an actress. She wants to be a star. She is calling a major regional theatre.

OLIVE

Is this Huntington Theatre Company? My name is Olive Allen. Did you write that down? Thank you…yes, I'm calling because I need an audition with you… Yes, yes, I know, I did send a picture and resume, but you don't get it – I really need this audition. …Well, because I'm a talent, that's why. And I'll have you know that Harold Prince is a friend of mine. I met him in a taxi in New York City once. Harold Prince! He's called Hal in the New York Times. He stole my taxi from me – I mean, how rude! It was raining and he said he needed a ride fast. I had to hail another cab … Well, ah…I was in a Girl Scout pageant when I was ten – but that was only as an amateur – and I sang in my church choir. I was excellent. My mother cried. …My aunt wrote play reviews for the Worcester Sentinel. She really knew her stuff, too. Never hesitated to say when something was crap. There's a ditzy little girl who's playing there at the Huntington now, the part of a hooker. I met her last week. She was kind enough to tell me, a woman of experience, that I could easily get an audition with you. Let me tell you, I'm better than her! I could play a hooker, no problem. After all I've been married eight years, I do know a little about sex. Hey, I can come in today, or tomorrow, or any day next week. I have a coach! I really do! He's an expert, trust me. Knows the meaning of the word "theatrical." (Pause) Look, just give me the audition, will you? I promise I'll be good. ...Oh, please, please, please? Listen - you don't know what talent is 'til you've seen me. I can cry on cue, I can slam a door, I can slap a cheating husband. And I know Ophelia. ... No, no, you don't get it! I've wanted to do this all my life! I've prepared the speech of Ophelia from *Hamlet* – and if I do say so, I look much younger than my real age! ...Oh, my God! You mean I can do it? An audition! That's just great, just great. ... Thursday at 10:00 am is kind of early. I'm usually eating toast and coffee at that hour. But I will be there. With my headshot and everything! Thank you so much! And by the way, I watch the Oscars every year. And the Tony's. And the Golden Globes. So I know good acting, believe me! I'll do you proud! Thank you!

(Hangs up.)

Jesus Christmas! What do you know? Anyone who doesn't know the meaning of persistence never met *me*.

36 HOURS
Amy Witting

Dramatic
Annie, thirty-two

Annie is speaking to Patrick Benton, 49. Annie and Patrick have reunited in a hotel room at Heathrow Airport after meeting for thirty-six hours years before in NYC. Patrick is the only person Annie has every really opened up to about the suicide of a man she loved. Here, in this monologue, she is explaining to Patrick how she wanted to give up but knowing that he was still somewhere in the world thinking of her convinced her, if only for a moment, to live.

ANNIE

I got a chair, rope, and I wrote five letters.
(She gets up and fishes through her backpack for the letters.)
One for Steven, one for my baby brother Maximilian, one for my parents, one for my best friend Tess, and look here. Look at this, one for a man that lives in Dorchester, England who I only met for thirty six hours, and this letter, this letter was the hardest to write. I was at my apartment, the one I told Steven I had rented out, the only place that feels like an untouchable heaven. I put them by my front door, the letters. The rope was tied nicely on the top of my closet. I bought it across the street at J&J hardware. I thought. I thought J&J might care enough to question the rope, but they didn't care. I first put it around my wrist. A knife in one hand and a noose, a practice noose in my other hand, and I did a test run. It burned like hell on my wrist, my writing arm. Clearly I wasn't thinking so I smoked a joint that Tess had left me in case of emergency, I put the letters down and stood on my black chair with the

green cushion wondering if it would just be fields of light that would first come and then a room full of those I loved waiting for me, led by him. His arms wrapping me tight, but also not tight at the same time since we would be in heaven. I imagined everything lighter in heaven. I stood high above the apartment I called my own and wanted complete darkness but there was my glaring computer screen so I came down with the intention of shutting it off and then shutting myself off, but there was your name in my inbox. Patrick Michael Benton, a name that haunts me. Patrick Michael Benton very much alive and breathing and just like that I decided to live.

For information on this author,
click on the WRITERS tab at www.smithandkraus.com.

THIS IS HOW YOU GOT ME NAKED
Catherine Weingarten

Comic
Jackie, 19

Jackie is at the Dress to Get Laid sex themed party at her college and all she wants is to win over her male dancer friend, Alaska. Her best friend Monday convinces her that the only way to get Alaska to date her is for them to have sex. In the beginning of this scene she finally gets to Alaska's room and is hoping to make something happen, but then he has to use the bathroom. In this comedic and cathartic monologue, Jackie has a real moment where she is finally able to process all the chaos of the party and tell him how she feels...even though he's not there.

JACKIE

Ugh I don't know how to do this at all. I really um *like* you... I think, I mean just the way you talk not like you as a person, ya know? Mostly cause like you talk so normally and I find that really cool. Like how did you even get here?? Like are you at the wrong school? Neva mind, I'm thinking too much. This party is relly cool! Like as a freshman and stuff I feel like honored cause like this party is for like people to like pursue me and want to jump me and that sounds like fulfilling and stuff. Like it's so crazy that upperclassmen have to wait till October for this party to like jump freshmen. I know I'm wearing like something kinda normal and most girls are wearing like bras and cellophane and have hot men's faces on their chests. I hope that's ok. You know I think it's really cool you're a junior?? Llike I *loved* your slam poetry performance on the topic of marshmallows. So simple yet like kinda hot, ya know? Like who thinks about marshmallows that much, like I don'. I just like eat them. Maybe I shouldn't have come to this party. But Monday said it would be fun and important for women. And now I'm in your room ,we're in this room together alone, well you are in your bathroom right now-so the adjacent room. Did you see downstairs there was like a pic of two chicks making out on the ceiling??

(It's all a little much.)

Fuck I think I'm crying, No wait I'm fine! I just have been taking this Meisner acting class for non-majors and all you do is talk about your childhood and shit and it's relly like opened me up and made me cry like all the time, pretty cool. I might leave…Should I be like on drugs or something to do this party right? Have I failed at living? Like you seem all calm and stuff like all the time…I think I love you…I mean not you, like um the concept of you, like you're worth crying about in Meisner. Fuck I like you so much.

THREE LADIES OF ORPINGTON
Daniel Guyton

Seriocomic
Maude, seventies

Maude is an elderly British woman from the Victorian Era. Here, she confronts the two men who have been plotting against her family.

MAUDE

You're all feeble minded! The entire lot of you!
(She cackles.)
And you may think that I don't recognize you, Mr. Babcock, but I do. Oh yes, I remember you clear as day. And you too, Mr. Fennimore! You both think me an old foolish woman, now don't you? But you're just a bunch of old wolves from back in the day. Oh yes, you've known each other for quite some now, haven't you? Yes, I dare say you have. And quite a team you two make. Quite a team indeed. One corrupts the lives of innocents, and the other one finishes the job. But if you believe my granddaughter will be as easy to corrupt as her mother was, "Lord Babcock," then you are quite mistaken. Oh yes. And you too, Mr. Fennimore. You may think you've outfoxed us all with your clever ruse, but you've both met your match in Elenore Dumpy, I can assure you of that. And as for you, Mr. Babcock… Pah! "Lord," my left foot. You're no more a lord than I am the queen of England! You've chosen the wrong household to return to, my dear boy. You left here many, many years ago, and I daresay you'll rue the day you ever decided to return. My granddaughter… Oh yes, my *granddaughter* will make you wish you had never been born. A lord. Ha! You wouldn't be a lord if you owned a million acres.

THREE LADIES OF ORPINGTON
Daniel Guyton

Dramatic
Henrietta, mid to late forties

Henrietta is an upper-class British woman from the Victorian era. Here, she explains to her daughter how she feels about men.

HENRIETTA

Oh. My dear child. Men are like eggs. If you leave them in the water too long, they can become hard and unmalleable. Or they can be soft and tender, if you break them early enough. But Mr. Babcock appears to have been left out in the sun too long. He's turned rotten. Oh, they believe that they are the center of the universe. That we must sit on them. And... coddle them. And warm them when they're chilly. And protect their fragile feelings from the outside elements. I was in love with another man once, Elenore. Before your father. I loved him with every fiber of my being. I gave myself to him. I... gave him everything I was. Everything I... knew I was. But his father discovered us. Lord Chesterfield Babcock the Elder. He found us in his son's bedroom. Engaged in ... He called me a harlot. And he had me thrust out of his castle gates like a common street whore. I had no wagon with me. No shoes on my feet. I had left them on the floor in Lord Chesterfield's bedroom. I had to walk. For nearly two days. With my soles exposed. Until one of our neighbors found me. Took me back home the rest of the way. That weekend, I heard the news. That Lord Chesterfield the Younger was... betrothed. Your grandfather never said a word about it. Never treated me unkind. Although I'm... sure I disappointed him terribly. Your grandmama, well... she helped me to arrange the marriage with your father. Those were very trying times, those days. So much... desperation. I look back now and wonder, what on earth did I ever see in that beast? He could have battled his father! He could have wrestled off the yoke of societal obligation, and fought his way back to me! To my arms! To my…bedchamber. To my soul's desire. But instead, he married her. Absconded off into the distance with my heart. What kind of person doesn't fight for the one he loves? Hmmm? What kind of person? It isn't a woman, Elenore. I can tell you that much. Because a woman fights! When it comes to love, a woman fights. A woman fights.

THREE LADIES OF ORPINGTON
Daniel Guyton

Dramatic
Elenore, 16

*Elenore is a British woman in the Victorian Era. Here,
she confronts the man who broke her heart.*

ELENORE

No. You may scowl at me to your pleasure, Mr. Babcock. But
my heart is mine to give. It isn't yours. I would have given my
heart to you, you know. Your words of flattery, and... love.
The music of your poetry hid the poison of your meaning, and
I was... far too dumb to understand it. Struck dumb by your...
elaborate deception. I may not be a beauty, Mr. Babcock. I
know this now. I have known this my entire life. But for a
fleeting instant, I believed that... for a fleeting moment, I believed that I had something beautiful inside of me. Something
beautiful that you, and only you alone, could see. And I allowed myself... I allowed myself to *feel*. (Pause) You don't
understand women, do you, Mr. Babcock? You don't... understand
people. Of any ilk. Do you? Do you understand what makes
us human? It is not money, or... inheritance. Or even our fancy titles. It's love. The ability to love. The capacity to love. I
love my mother very much. And my grandmother. And for a
moment... For a fleeting instant, I believed that I loved you.
But you have disappointed me greatly, Mr. Babcock. You have
destroyed my trust in love. This heart belonged to me. But you
have stolen it from me, for just a moment. For just a fleeting,
insignificant second, in your eyes. But knowing that my heart
was ever yours ... was ever *owned* by such a cold and calculating
fiend ... that this beating heart within my ribs could ever flip so
casually to the whims of such as beast as you. It makes me
HATE my heart, Mr. Babcock! It makes me HATE that I ever

loved! It makes me HATE that this foul contraption could ever live inside my body! So if you have any compassion left inside you, Mr. Babcock; if you have any love or kindness left inside of you, you will split me open with that hatchet. You will remove the offending organ from behind my breasts, and you will crush my detestable heart in front of me! Do it! Now. Once, and for bloody all.

TURN! TURN! TURN!
Bara Swain

Comic
Diane, 30s-40s

*During a sound check at a funeral, self-centered
Diane expresses her concern that her marriage is
over to her cousin.*

DIANE

HEY, CAN SOMEBODY TURN THAT DAMNED MUSIC
OFF? (Beat) Sure, sure, it'll be over in a minute. Like stirrup pants
were over in a minute. Like scrunchies and rice necklaces were over
in a minute! LIKE MY MARRIAGE WAS OVER IN A MINUTE!
All I said was, "Benji, I made dinner reservations at the Rainbow
Room for our wedding anniversary next Sunday. They're serving
chicken and truffle pot pies." That's his favorite, and he says, "I'll
be out of town on a business trip." What the fuck? Insensitive, cruel,
and indifferent, am I right? "You want to go away on Election Day,
Benji? Bon fucking-voyage. You need to go on a business trip on
Chinese New Year, Benji? Sayo-fuckin-nara." But *this*, Janet, this
is our anniversary. If that's not sacred, what is? Oh, I know what
you're thinking. I know exactly what you're thinking. Life is sacred. Life with a capital "L" is sacred. And now you're going to
make me feel guilty because I'm mourning the end of my marriage
while Cousin Whatever-the-Hell-His-Name-Is is lying a hundred
yards away in a plain wooden box because – and I'm not afraid
to say it – because his devoted wife of more than fifty years is too
cheap to buy mahogany or walnut, or pay for cable TV! Sure, and
when I see Cousin Bertha eating eggs benedict with a double side
of bacon, *then* we can have this discussion again.

For information on this author,
click on the WRITERS tab at www.smithandkraus.com.

VINO VERITAS
David MacGregor

Comic
Claire, 30s-40s

*After imbibing a tribal truth serum, sweet and inno-
cent housewife Claire begins to reveal her innermost
thoughts to her bewildered husband.*

CLAIRE

Ridley's mother? Please. Any time she comes over to our
house it's like inviting a killer whale to a baby seal festival. It's
just carnage as far as the eye can see. I mean, she's babysitting
tonight, right? Do you know what she brought over for Kris-
ta? Three brand new DVDs. And not just any DVDs, oh no.
Winnie the Pooh. Yep. You heard me right. Winnie the fucking
Pooh. What? Oh my God…you don't get it, do you? Well, of
course you don't. You're all adults and leading adult lives and
talking about drywall and the price of gas and whatnot. So,
let me ask you something. This is a serious question. Have
you ever watched Winnie the Pooh? I mean, really watched it?
Because I know Ridley hasn't. He's too busy with his patients
and clinics and classes and seminars and I'm the one who sits
at home watching Winnie the Pooh over and over until every
detail of The Goddamned Hundred Acre Wood is burned into
the back of my retinas! Excuse me? You want to talk to me
about Winnie the Pooh? Is that what you're saying? I'll tell
you about Winnie the fucking Pooh. Winnie the Pooh is an
obsessive-compulsive addict who will do anything to score his
next fix. They say it's honey he's after, but it might as well
be crack or crystal meth. He talks about it, he sings about it,
he thinks about it every minute of every day. His best friend
Piglet? Neurotic and latently gay. Why else would he have a
picture of Pooh on his living room wall? Eeyore? That poor

son of a bitch loses body parts on a regular basis and is badly in need of some antidepressants. Owl is utterly delusional, Rabbit is a control freak, Gopher has a horrible speech impediment, Tigger is a classic case for the benefits of Ritalin, and I'll tell you right now, I think Roo is just a little bit too old to be hanging out in Kanga's pouch! The Hundred Acre Wood is like some kind of cartoon mental institution! And that's the kind of movie your mother brings into our home.

.

For information on this author,
click on the WRITERS tab at www.smithandkraus.com.

VINO VERITAS
David MacGregor

Dramatic
Lauren, 30s-40s

Lauren shares the darkest moment of her life with close friends who thought they knew everything about her.

LAUREN

You want to hear about a day that changed everything? Brandon and Zack had a little sister. They did. Or at least, they were going to have one. And the reason you don't know about it is because we never told anyone. We were waiting until after the ultrasound to make the big announcement. But then, the ultrasound didn't go too well. And all the tests after that went even worse. That's when we learned the secret that they don't tell you in the baby books or the classes…that if a baby is too damaged, the doctors will take care of it for you. Oh no. No, we didn't have an abortion. God forbid it should be called an abortion. No, in cases like ours, the doctors have a special magic phrase they use, just to make everyone feel better. It's not an abortion…it's a medical interruption. So, we signed the papers, all the papers, and then they wheeled me down the hallway into this small little room. Phil was there the whole time holding my hand, and all we could do was look at one another…because we couldn't even speak. Then the doctor took a long needle, and he filled that needle with potassium chloride. Then he took that needle and put it through my stomach, and right into our baby daughter's tiny heart. And then the doctor said, "The baby's heart has stopped." Now that's a day that changed everything. So go ahead, Ridley. Tell Phil he's never stared into the abyss...tell me I haven't. And then let me tell you something. The tragedy isn't that it happened to us. The tragedy is that it's always happening to someone, somewhere. Right now, a mother is waking up and wondering why her newborn didn't cry once all night. Right now, someone's getting a call telling them the biopsy results look bad. That's what's so easy for us to forget…that every day is a day that changes everything for someone…and that's what we need to remember.

For information on this author,
click on the WRITERS tab at www.smithandkraus.com.

WASHER/DRYER
Nandita Shenoy

Comic
Sonya, mid-30s

Sonya has been hiding a secret from her new husband, Michael. She hasn't told him that her studio apartment in a Manhattan co-op is single occupancy only even though he has moved in with her because she doesn't want to give up her washer/dryer. As multiple revelations threaten to upend their newlywed bliss, Michael pushes Sonya too far on the topic of her beloved appliance.

SONYA

You don't understand my fucking washer-dryer? Do you know how I bought this place? I had my face on the side of a Monistat box for three years! Three years when my disembodied head sailed through the air on morning television extolling the virtues of a three-day suppository. Three years when at every party I went to someone would ask me if I was having that "not so fresh" feeling even though that is the line from a Summer's Eve commercial and has nothing to do with Monistat at all. But the money was good. It was so good that I didn't care. And somewhere in my mind, a little voice said, "This might be as good as it gets." So instead of going hog wild on residuals, I saved it all up for a down payment on an apartment so that I could have a home, always. I looked at 42 apartments all by myself, made offers on four, but this is the only one that accepted. The horrible board made me jump through all kinds of hoops with letters of reference and pages and pages of documents. They practically asked me for my first-born child. My face broke out from the stress. But at the end of it all, single Indian actress me owned a small, very small, piece of real estate on the isle of Manhattan which contained the ultimate prize for any New York apartment hunter–a washer-dryer. And even though it's small and in a ridiculous building, this apartment is everything to me. It is the house that yeast built. And if you don't understand that, Mr. Momma's Boy, then we should not be married at all.

WOMEN IN JEOPARDY
Wendy MacLeod

Comic
Liz, 40s-early 50s

Liz, a middle-aged divorcee, has brought her new dentist boyfriend over to meet her best friends, Mary and Jo. Mary and Jo, who are also divorced and single, have escaped to the kitchen to refill the hummus and to privately agree that Jackson is kind of a weirdo. Liz follows them and encourages them to come back and give Jackson a chance.

LIZ

It's just he's out there, you know. His sense of humor. He is just so out there. So I totally understand if you don't "get" him. But you will. His hygienists love him. Love him. It's a very successful practice. I mean let's face it a dentist is...a dentist is a doctor. Women are always desperate to marry doctors. Why not dentists? They're doctors who work regular hours I said to him, I said Jackson, why did you never marry? Why weren't you snatched up? You who were so successful and sexy and funny? I'm looking for the corkscrew. You must have noticed how my body is changing...My hair is shinier, my lips are plumper, I'm lubricated, my hips swivel when I walk. You can actually feel the heat coming off me!

There has been a renaissance of my nether parts! My desire has grown so fierce that I can't think of anything else! Sometimes Jackson and I actually weep together over the years we spent apart, when I was just one of those dateless divorced women in sensible shoes doing Fun Runs and book clubs. Don't give up hope girls! Your Jackson is out there somewhere!

Rights & Permissions

(NOTE: To obtain the entire text of a play, contact the rights holder or, when indicated, the publisher.)

ACTUALLY © 2017 by Anna Ziegler. Reprinted by permission of Seth Glewen Gersh Agency. For performance rights, contact Dramatists Play Service, 440 Park Ave. S., New York, NY 10016 (212-683-8960) (www.dramatists.com)

AIRNESS © 2017 by Chelsea Marcantel. Reprinted by permission of Amy Mellman, ICM Partners. For performance rights, contact Di Glazer, ICM Partners, dglazer@icmpartners.com

ALL THE RAGE © 2017 by Joshua James. Reprinted by permission of Joshua James. For performance rights, contact Joshua James, joshuajames99@yahoo.com

AMY AND THE ORPHANS © 2017 by Lindsey Ferrentino. Reprinted by permission of Ally Shuster, Creative Artists Agency. For performance rights, contact Ally Shuster, ally.shuster@caa.com

AND THEN THEY FELL © 2016 by Tira Palmquist. Reprinted by permission of Susan Gurman, Susan Gurman Agency LLC. For performance rights, contact Susan Gurman, susan@gurmanagency.com

ANIMAL © 2017 by Clare Lizzimore. Reprinted by permission of Rachel Taylor Casarotto, Ramsay & Assoc. Ltd. For performance rights, contact Rachel Taylor, rtaylor@casarotto.co.uk The entire text is published by Oberon Books Ltd., www.oberonbooks.com

EVERYTHING IS WONDERFUL © 2017 by Chelsea Marcantel. Reprinted by permission of Amy Mellman, ICM Partners. For performance rights, contact Di Glazer, ICM Partners, dglazer@icmpartners.com

FERNANDO © 2017 by Steven Haworth. Reprinted by permission of Steven Haworth. For performance rights, contact Steven Haworth, stevencharleshaworth@yahoo.com

FIRE IN DREAMLAND © 2017 by Rinne Groff. Reprinted by permission of Chris Till, Creative Artists Agency. For performance rights, contact Chris Till, ctill@caa.com

FLYING LEAP © 2017 by Anton Dudley. Reprinted by permission of Anton Dudley. For performance rights, contact Anton Dudley, antondudley@gmail.com

HAPPY BIRTHDAY, MOM © 2017 by Meghan Gambling. Reprinted by permission of Meghan Gambling. For performance rights, contact Meghan Gambling, meggamster@gmail.com

HIPPOPOTAMUS © 2017 by Libby Emmonds. Reprinted by permission of Libby Emmons. For performance rights, contact Libby Emmons, blueboxworld@gmail.com

THE HOMELESS SECRETARY © 2017 by Gerry Sheridan. Reprinted by permission of Gerry Sheridan. For performance rights, contact Gerry Sheridan, gerrysheridan@earthlink.net

HOW TO TRANSCEND A HAPPY MARRIAGE © 2017 by Sarah Ruhl. Reprinted by permission of Mark Subias United Talent Agency. For performance rights, contact Samuel French, Inc., 212-206-8990, www.samuelfrench.com

HUNGRY © 2017 by Kayla Cagan. Reprinted by permission of Kayla Cagan. For performance rights, contact Kayla Cagan, kayla.cagan@gmail.com

HURRICANE; or Clap your Hands If You Remember Tower Records © 2017 by Brooke Berman. Reprinted by permission of Brooke Berman. For performance rights, contact Brooke Berman, brookeberman@gmail.com

IN SERVICE OF VENUS © 2018 by Anna Wilcoxen. Reprinted by permission of Anna Wilcoxen. For performance rights, contact Anna Wilcoxen, annawilcoxen@gmail.com

INVINCIBLE © 2014 by Torben Betts. Reprinted by permission of Oberon Books Ltd.. For performance rights, contact lucy@oberonbooks.com

KIDNAP ROAD © 2017 by Catherine Filloux. Reprinted by permission of Catherine Filloux. For performance rights, Elaine Devlin, Elaine Devlin Literary, edevlinlit@aol.com

KISS © 2017 by Guillermo Calderón. Reprinted by permission of Antje Oegel, AO International Agency. For performance rights, contact Antje Oegel, aoegel@aoiagency.com

KITCHEN SINK DRAMA © 2017 by Andrew Biss. Reprinted by permission of Andrew Biss. For performance rights, contact Andrew Biss, andrewbiss@gmail.com

KODACHROME © 2017 by Adam Szymkowicz. Reprinted by permission of Seth Glewen, Gersh Agency. For performance rights, contact Seth Glewen, sglewen@gershny.com

THE LACY PROJECT © 2017 by Alena Smith. Reprinted by permission of Ally Shuster, Creative Artists Agency. For perfor-